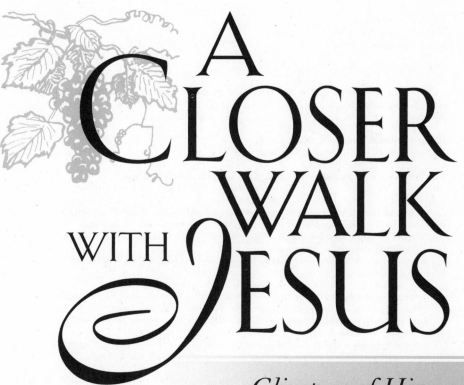

A CLOSER WALK WITH JESUS

Glimpses of Him in Everyday Life

Edited by
Evelyn Bence

GuidepostsBooks®
New York, New York

GuidepostsBooks·

A Closer Walk with Jesus

ISBN 978-0-8249-4729-3

Published by GuidepostsBooks
16 East 34ᵗʰ Street, New York, New York 10016
www.guidepostsbooks.com

Copyright © 2007 by GuidepostsBooks. All rights reserved.

This book, or parts thereof, may not be reproduced, stored in a retrieval system, or transmitted in any form or by any means, electronic, mechanical, photocopying, recording or otherwise, without the written permission of the publisher.

Distributed by Ideals Publications, a Guideposts company
535 Metroplex Drive, Suite 250, Nashville, Tennessee 37211

GuidepostsBooks and *Ideals* are registered trademarks of Guideposts, Carmel, New York.

ACKNOWLEDGMENTS

Every attempt has been made to credit the sources of copyrighted material used in this book. If any such acknowledgment has been inadvertently omitted or miscredited, receipt of such information would be appreciated.

All material that originally appeared in *Angels on Earth, Daily Guideposts, Guideposts* and *The Guideposts Home Bible Study Program* is reprinted with permission.

Scripture quotations marked (AMP) are taken from *The Amplified Bible*, © 1965 by Zondervan Publishing House. All rights reserved.

Scripture quotations marked (KJV) are taken from *The King James Version of the Bible*.

Scripture quotations marked (NIV) are taken from *The Holy Bible, New International Version*. Copyright © 1973, 1978, 1984 International Bible Society. Used by permission of Zondervan Bible Publishers.

Scripture quotations marked (NKJV) are taken from *The Holy Bible, New King James Version*. Copyright © 1997, 1990, 1985, 1983 by Thomas Nelson, Inc.

Scripture quotations marked (RSV) are taken from the *Revised Standard Version of the Bible*. Copyright ©1946, 1952, 1971 by Division of Christian Education of the National Council of Churches of Christ in the U.S.A. Used by permission.

"A Vision of Glory" taken from *Spiritual Moments with the Great Hymns* by Evelyn Bence. Copyright © 1997 by Evelyn Bence. Used by permission of the Zondervan Corporation.

"Jesus and Joy: A Picture in the Wallet of My Heart" from *Champagne for the Soul* by Mike Mason, Regent College Publishing, Vancouver. Copyright © 2007 by Mike Mason.

"Jesus in Each One of Them" is excerpted from *God's Forever Feast* by Paul Brand. Copyright © 1993 by Paul Brand. Reprinted with permission from Discovery House Publishers, Grand Rapids, MI 49512. All rights reserved.

"My Easter Story" from *Celebrate Joy!* by Velma Seawell Daniels. Copyright © 1981 by Velma Seawell Daniels. Reprinted with permission by the author.

Library of Congress Cataloging-in-Publication Data

A closer walk with Jesus : glimpses of him in everyday life.
    p. cm.
  ISBN 978-0-8249-4729-3
  1. Jesus Christ—Person and offices. 2. Spirituality. I. Guideposts Associates.
  BT203.C56 2007
  232—dc22
                    2007007370

Jacket photo © Victoria Pearson/Botanica/JupiterImages
Jacket and interior design by Marisa Jackson

Printed and bound in the United States of America

10 9 8 7 6 5 4 3 2 1

TABLE OF CONTENTS

INTRODUCTION

Just a closer walk with Thee,
Grant it, Jesus, is my plea.

As a teenager I loved this gospel song by William Floyd. Though it wasn't in our church hymnals, it was so familiar—soulfully sung by Elvis Presley and Stuart Hamblin. The song helped me personalize a scriptural image. . . .

Walking with God. It's an ancient phrase used to describe Adam in the Garden of Eden and later, in the book of Genesis, Enoch and Noah—people who were especially aware of and attuned to God's presence.

Then in the New Testament we get a sense of people *walking with Jesus.* As I read the Gospel accounts, it's easy to envision sandaled Jesus, surrounded by disciples, trekking from one village to another. I think of Him sometimes teaching, sometimes listening intently, sometimes simply being *present* among them, maybe singing old-time songs of Zion.

Jesus' most memorable walk with friends was after His Resurrection, on the road from Jerusalem to the village of Emmaus. Mysteriously, His friends didn't recognize Him immediately. And in this way they are much like us today—though Jesus is present in our midst, on our daily walk, do we appreciate or understand who or where He is? Do we glimpse Him walking with us on the road of life?

Eight hundred years ago an English bishop, Richard of Chichester, wrote a prayer that is still relevant and even popular today, ever since its inclusion in the musical *Godspell*, a 1970's sensation. It perfectly ties together the two threads in this book—glimpsing and also walking with our Lord. As you settle your spirit and set out on this reading adventure, I suggest you focus on Richard's prayer, making it your own:

> O most merciful Redeemer, Friend, and Brother, may I
> see thee more clearly, love thee more dearly, and follow
> thee more nearly, day by day.

We've collected the true stories in this volume because of the way they illustrate how men, women, even children—some devout, some searching—have glimpsed Jesus in various roles: as Friend, as Savior, as Lord, as Healer, as Guide and Leader, as Mentor and Model, as Strength for the journey. One of my favorite stories is by Rulon Gardner. While holding the Olympic gold medal for heavyweight wrestling—by some counts the strongest man in the world—he had a dream of Jesus, which grounded his view of Jesus as the Strength of his life.

We often learn spiritual lessons—how to draw closer to Jesus, how to see Him more clearly—as we see His work unfold in other people's lives. That's why this book contains primarily personal stories. But sprinkled throughout, especially in the shorter pieces, are some very practical pointers for keeping in step with, in sight of, Jesus. That's what you'll find in such chapters as "My Worry Window" by Sue Monk Kidd, "Then I Remembered" by Keith Miller and also in "A Final Word," a chapter called "A Pilgrim's Ascent."

As I found and sorted stories for inclusion, I knew that a "closer walk" collection would not be complete without Margaret Powers' story that tells the circumstances behind her writing the poem "Footprints," which circulated widely for years without any author attribution. You may remember the setting—at the end of his life a man dreams he's been walking with

Jesus along a beach. The man realizes that sometimes—during the most stressful days—there were only one set of footprints in the sand, not two. *Why—what's this about?* the dreamer asks Jesus. Jesus' response? Well, turn the page and read Margaret's story of her dream of Jesus, which, in turn, introduces the rest of the book, in which we glimpse the presence and work of Jesus in some of His many roles and see how others have walked ever so near to Him.

FOOTPRINTS IN THE SAND

by Margaret Rose Powers

I was only in my twenties, but I knew if I lived to be one hundred twenty I'd never be sadder than I was the summer of 1964. I was recuperating at our family farmhouse in Tillsonburg, Ontario. Meningitis kept me in and out of bed most of the summer; my small frame shrank to eighty-five pounds. But I wondered too how much my fevered emotions had prolonged my illness. A relationship I'd clung to had finally come apart, and I was brokenhearted.

Friends always called me a hopeless romantic; now I felt only hopeless. Thoughts of couples walking along the nearby Lake Erie shore made me even lonelier. I missed that safe feeling I once knew, walking barefoot on the beach with someone you love, the sand reaching ahead as far as you can see, the great lake stretching into the horizon. It's a perfect, peaceful feeling.

But that feeling had betrayed me. I could never trust it again. "I've never felt so empty and afraid," I wrote in my diary one August evening. "Lord, have You left me too?"

When the phone rang the third time, I put down my pen. My brother Jim beckoned me to come visit him in Pickering, twenty miles outside of Toronto. As we chatted, I leafed through the inked pages of my diary, filled with poems I'd been composing for years. Jim said he remembered my earliest verse, scrawled on handmade birthday cards when we were kids. Maybe spending some time with my brother would do me some good.

Jim understood that I wasn't quite up to socializing, so we did quiet things together. That is, until we bumped into his old friend Paul Powers in downtown Toronto. Jim mentioned that we were headed to the Honeydew Restaurant for dinner.

"My favorite! Mind if I tag along?" Paul asked us both without taking his eyes off me.

I looked pleadingly at Jim just as he said, "Why not?"

At the restaurant, Paul asked me a million questions—personal questions. Jim sensed my unease and steered the conversation to Paul. He was a youth minister who liked to use magic illusions to entertain and challenge young people. It was easy to imagine Paul at work; he was confident and certainly didn't lack dramatic flair. He told stories about traveling all over Ontario and Quebec, and made one coin after another disappear into a napkin. But every time he got serious and spoke in his soft voice, his big blue eyes held mine until I looked away.

Had my dear brother put him up to this? Or did Paul just feel sorry for me? Most of my dinner stayed on my plate, and Paul finished my dessert.

As we were leaving, Paul boldly asked if he could take me to the "Ex"—Toronto's annual Canadian National Exhibition—the next day. A date? I fumbled for an excuse. There was something sweet about this fellow, even if he was a tad earnest. *You need a day out*, I rationalized. But that would be it. *Just a day out.* "You'll never regret saying yes," Paul promised, the excitement in his eyes nearly convincing me I wouldn't.

Paul was an hour late, and in that time I tried to tell myself that all of his interest in me was just show. But I also kept changing my outfit. Paul arrived finally (he'd gotten lost), and we drove to "the world's largest fair" only to find that a drenching downpour had turned the exhibition grounds parking lot into a bog.

Paul got out of the car, sloshed over to the passenger side, and saw me hesitate, my feet dangling over a muddy puddle. In an instant, he swept me up in his strong arms. I thought I would die of embarrassment. In the distance wide-striped carnival tents billowed in the wind, the Ferris wheel peeping out over one of them. Band music grew louder as we neared the ticket booth, Paul carrying me all the way.

He wanted to go on every ride. He was lively and tender all at the same time. I never knew quite what to expect out of him. Still, I felt inexplicably drawn to him. He was so sure of himself. After the evening concert, when he asked if I would see him again, I found myself laughing and replying coyly, "I'll consider it." And when we kissed good night I knew I would.

I closed the door, kicked off my muddy shoes and twirled onto my bed. What were these giddy feelings? *You hardly know Paul. You'll only get hurt again. We would be friends,* I decided. *That's all.*

Paul's work kept him busy, but we wrote lots of letters. Once I mailed three in a single day! Eventually I found myself revealing more to him than I'd ever imagined wanting to. I told him things about myself I'd never told anyone. We really were becoming friends, close friends.

One month later, in early autumn, we had another date, this time in Kingston, where Paul was speaking at a youth retreat. "The Lake Ontario beach is breathtaking this time of year," Paul said with the enthusiasm I'd grown so fond of. But I was more nervous than ever. *What did I want to happen between us?*

The moment I saw Paul, I knew he had something on his mind. Then he drew a small black box from his inside jacket pocket, and opened it. Nestled in velvet was a sparkling diamond engagement ring. "I love you," he said.

I looked at the ring, looked at Paul, gasped. This wasn't supposed to happen. I'm not ready . . . "Paul," I stammered, "Paul, I can't . . ."

He put his finger to my lips and dropped the ring box back in his pocket. I knew he hadn't given up on me. But I was so confused . . .

The day flew by in a blur, and finally after hours of talking, we strolled quietly along the shore late in the afternoon. We took off our shoes and walked holding hands on the windswept beach. The waves hissed into bubbles at our feet. Paul stopped suddenly and pointed back at our tracks in the sand. "See our footprints, Margie? On the day we marry, they will become like one set, not two."

The poet in me stirred. *How could I let this man go? And yet how could I risk loving him?*

That night, the image of our footprints was still with me. I couldn't sleep. I filled pages of my diary. *Dear Lord,* I finally prayed, *where are You now, when I need You so badly?*

Then, as if in a dream, I saw a story unfolding in my mind's eye. My pen took over as I began writing it out. I saw myself walking along a beach with the Lord, and scenes from my life flashed before us. But during the most painful scenes, I noticed, only one set of footprints was left in the sand. I asked the Lord where He had been when I needed Him most. Then I wrote down His reply:

> "My precious child,
> I love you and will never leave you.
> When you saw only one set of footprints,
> It was then that I carried you."

I put down my pen beside the verse shaped on the page. It was almost as if I hadn't written it myself. But I knew this poem came from a place deep inside me, a place Paul had been able to reach. I remembered how he'd swept me up in his arms at the fair, when I was feeling so lonely and afraid. It could have been one of the painful scenes that had flashed before me in the dream I'd written the poem about. And then I knew: The Lord had been carrying me; He'd sent me Paul when I thought I could never trust love again. If we were to walk as one, as Paul had said, the Lord would carry us both through troubled times.

And suddenly, as I reread the poem, I felt myself being swept up in the Lord's arms, lifted above my fears and hurt. And I let God's perfect love heal me so I could love again. And then I knew what my answer to Paul would be.

THE STORY BEHIND THE STORY

by John Ballard

For years I kept a copy of "Footprints" tacked on the wall behind my desk at the Cedar Grove Counseling Center in Surrey, British Columbia. Its author was listed as "unknown." One day a friend happened to mention that the author wasn't unknown at all. In fact, her name was Margaret Powers and she lived not far away, in the town of Coquitlam.

I had to meet this writer, if only to tell her of the many people I counseled who had been helped by the message of her beautiful parable—and to learn how "Footprints" could have gone unattributed for all those years. So I took a drive over to Coquitlam, spent an afternoon with Margaret Powers and learned the story behind my favorite poem.

Margaret Fishback and Paul Powers were married the summer after they met. They raised two daughters. Over the years the poem she put in her diary called "The Dream," with its enduring footprints image, was passed among her friends and family. She never published her poem, but she did make copies for people who requested it. The poem began to spread throughout Canada and, much to Margaret's amazement, the world. It was translated into dozens of languages, printed on coffee mugs and key chains and given a new title—"Footprints." Somehow Margaret Powers' name was lost.

People who knew her urged Margaret to claim her authorship. "It's your work!" they pleaded. But by then, in the course of several moves, she'd lost all her early handwritten versions of "The Dream," which she felt would show that she had composed the poem.

Then one day in 1983 Margaret Powers saw her "anonymous" poem printed on a poster of a sandy shore. It could have been the very same sandy Lake Ontario beach she had walked along with Paul Powers on the day he proposed. Something in her stirred. "Mom," she told her mother in a call that night, "I took Paul Powers' name because of that poem. Sometimes I wish I could see the Powers name on 'Footprints.'"

"Margie, that's it!" her mother blurted out. "Your wedding album! I remember your sitting down and writing the poem in that album just before your wedding!"

Margaret went up in the attic and found the album with the poem she had written in it so many years before. Eventually that album was one of the things that convinced Hallmark Cards to attribute "Footprints" to M. R. Powers.

I have a new version of "Footprints" hanging behind my desk. This one has the author's name on it. In fact, she signed it herself the day I went out to see her.

PART 1

Glimpses of Jesus
as Friend and Companion

"I no longer call you servants . . . .
Instead, I have called you friends. . . ."
—JESUS, JOHN 15:15 (NIV)

OUR FIRST STORIES PROVIDE A CLEAR SETTING in which we can picture Jesus' presence alongside the narrators—walking, traveling, chatting—as a friend and companion.

The Easter theme of Velma Daniels' story reminds me of the old song titled "In the Garden," written in the voice of Jesus' friend Mary Magdalene, describing her Easter morning encounter with Jesus:

I come to the garden alone,
While the dew is still on the roses. . . .
He speaks and the sound of his voice
Is so sweet the birds hush their singing. . . .
And he walks with me,
And he talks with me. . . .
—Austin Miles

Come, walk with us and discover the friendship Jesus offers, even now, even you.

OH, TO HAVE A FRIEND

by Helen Grace Lescheid

Forty years ago as a lonely immigrant girl in Canada, I had an experience so hard to describe that it took me many years even to try. Yet the story needs to be told, for it points up how intimately God knows His children.

That October day in 1952 as I listened to the lunchtime chatter in my high school homeroom, the ache in my throat made it hard to swallow my meal of dark rye bread. Won't I ever belong?

I was fifteen. Two years earlier I'd entered Lord Tweedsmuir High School in Surrey, British Columbia, a frightened newcomer from Germany. Shy and awkward anyway, I'd been too ashamed of my limited English to reply when someone spoke to me.

As the months went by my English improved, but my sense of belonging did not. Everything about me was different from these outgoing Canadian girls—my accent, my hand-me-down clothes, my thick blond braids (too beautiful to cut, my mother said when I pleaded that all the other girls wore their hair short). Even the lunch I brought from home: My classmates brought sandwiches on thin-sliced white bread; I had thick black rye and jam. I was the odd one, the outsider. In two years I'd made not a single friend.

I stuffed my uneaten lunch back inside my desk and fled from the happy babble of the classroom. Through crowded halls I pushed my way to the library. Books at least were my friends . . . but not that day. As I glanced up from reading, I saw through the window an ordinary scene. Two girls sat on the grass, heads together, talking. Such longing rose inside me I knew I was going to cry. Oh, to have a friend—just one friend with whom I could sit and talk that way!

I escaped from the library and dodged into the bathroom, where I could lock the door and let the tears come. "Lord Jesus, I'm so lonely!" To talk to Jesus was natural to me; I'd been taught that He cared for each of us personally. I'd gaze at paintings of Him, thinking how friendly He looked, how I'd have told Him anything if I'd lived back then.

After school I stood as usual at the bus stop on the fringe of a knot of schoolmates. One of the girls turned to me. "Helen, are you going to the school dance on Friday?" I shook my head no. "Why don't you come?" she coaxed.

I shut my eyes against a memory. At the last dance I'd stood on the sidelines for what seemed hours. At last a boy walked up to me—but what he did was yank one of my braids. Everyone had laughed. No, I'd never put myself through that again! The girl beside me fell silent, then turned back to the others.

I mounted the big yellow bus and scanned it for a seat by the window, where I could keep from meeting people's eyes. But the window seats were taken. I slumped down beside a girl who smiled at me. *She's friendly*, I thought. I'd like to say something friendly to her. I was too tongue-tied. Throughout the half-hour ride I said not a word.

Close to tears again, I stumbled off the bus and hurried into the old farmhouse. As usual our rented house was empty. Mother, who'd been widowed in World War II, worked up to ten hours in the vegetable fields each day to support herself and her four children. Come to think of it, my younger sisters and brother seemed to have no trouble making friends in our new country. They were probably off playing with the neighbor's kids at this very moment. It was me—something was terribly wrong with me.

Dropping my books on the kitchen table, I ran into the bedroom, slammed the door shut and fell across the bed. My body, so flat and long and lanky, shook with sobs.

I sat up abruptly. Someone else was in the room! Hastily wiping my eyes I looked around. Nobody. But—someone was here. I could feel it.

Not someone . . . Someone. There was an aura in that little room I could almost touch. Love such as I'd never felt before filled the space all around me. "Jesus," I whispered, "is that You?"

He answered, not with an audible voice, but with a love so tangible I felt hugged. Although I saw nothing physical, an image burned itself into my mind: a friendly face with smiling eyes, so vivid that even today, forty years later, I see them still. Eyes that danced . . . "You know what? I like you! You're my special friend!"

As I sat there on my bed, the glorious, gracious words kept coming: "Have you forgotten that you belong to Me? I will never leave you or forsake you. I'm here with you now and will always be with you. Don't be ashamed! I love you just as you are."

For a long time I sat there basking in love beyond my conceiving, hearing those words of unconditional acceptance. When my family came home they found me humming as I prepared supper.

The next morning I opened my eyes to find the joyful Presence still filling the room, as though He'd waited for me to wake up so we could start the day together. When I boarded the yellow bus He did too.

During class it was as though He were standing beside my desk. We did math problems together. We wrote essays together. Even in gym class, which I'd always dreaded, I could feel Him running beside me.

At lunch break that day one of my classmates asked me if I would help her with a problem. She hadn't understood the teacher and felt sure

I had. Wondering why she'd singled me out, yet thrilled that somebody had, I slid over and made room for her at my desk—not even trying to hide my dark chunk of bread.

Later at the bus stop I stood with the familiar cluster of teens. My Friend whispered, "Aren't they a great bunch of kids? I also love them dearly." I turned to stare at them with new appreciation. Friendly eyes met mine. Later that week some girls invited me to join the glee club and I eagerly accepted.

The fact that my peers now wanted to be with me never ceased to amaze me. One day one of my sisters hinted at the reason. "Helen, what's happened to you? You're always so happy now!" I looked at her in surprise. True, I was supremely happy, but I hadn't been aware it showed.

For three glorious months my Friend and I walked in this indescribable companionship. I had never felt so completely believed in and understood. He was always smiling at me, a big smile of delight and approval, and it was impossible not to smile back at the world around me. Every morning when I got up He was there. All day He walked beside me. In the evening my last awareness was of Him.

Then one dreadful morning I awoke to an empty room. The joyful Presence was gone. Panic seized me. "Jesus!" I cried. Silence. I must have sinned in some terrible way. Frantically I searched my conscience. I confessed every sin I could recall and begged Him to forgive my unknown ones. But the almost palpable sense of His presence did not return.

Grief-stricken, I opened my Bible. Where were those words Jesus had spoken to me three months before, right in this room? I found them in the thirteenth chapter of Hebrews: ". . . for He hath said, 'I will never leave thee, nor forsake thee'"(v. 5 KJV).

I saw the words, I believed the words. But I did not feel them—not the way I had before. Slowly I repeated the phrase, "I will never leave thee, nor forsake thee."

"Jesus, did You say never so that I might know today that You are still with me even though I don't feel You?" I whispered. This glimmer of hope in time became a growing reality: No matter how I feel, Jesus is always with me. His love and acceptance are a fact independent of my moods and feelings.

It was only much later that I understood the double gift Jesus gave to a clumsy immigrant girl. He came as a tangible Presence to assure me of my value in His sight, and to show me the value of friendship. Then He withdrew this special feeling. "You will find Me in My written Word," He seemed to be saying, "and in so many different ways." He stepped a little distance back, to make room for faith and character to grow. Isn't that what a best friend would do?

MY EASTER STORY

by Velma Daniels

Easter was explained to me first when I was six years old. I remember the day well—Easter Sunday 1938. But twenty-five years passed before the full meaning of that explanation became clear.

I am not talking about Easter as it is celebrated with chocolate bunnies or colored eggs or with a parade of new hats. I am thinking of Easter in a small faraway garden, nearly two thousand years ago. Because my Easter story began in a garden too—with a friend.

The garden belonged to "Miss Mary." And that was the day I met her and we became friends.

But I'm getting ahead of myself. Let me tell you how it began.

My family had just moved into a large new home. That is, it was a new home for us, but an old house on the edge of a small town in Central Florida. It stood in the middle of a large wooded lot. The circular drive was paved with nothing more than pine needles. Clustered against the house were all sorts of shrubs and bushes—not flowers.

But the house next door—what a difference!

You would call it a cottage, and it was completely surrounded by flowers. Some flowers blanketed parts of the yard, and others crept into corners or climbed up the trunks of the trees. Some of the blooms even towered over my head.

For the first few days in our new home, I stared at this strange place with the curiosity of any small child. I wondered about the woman in the big straw hat who seemed to be so busy all day long among her flowers.

Then came the first Sunday in our new home. After we had returned from church, my mother said, "While you are still dressed so pretty, why don't you visit that nice lady next door and get acquainted? I'll fix a gift for you to take to her."

So it was a few minutes later I walked up the path that led to the most colorful garden I have ever seen and to a conversation that changed the course of my life.

She was watering a bed of violets as I approached her timidly. "My name is Velma," I said as I handed her a plate of cookies. "We just moved next door, and my mother made these tea cakes for you."

She smiled and said, "I am Miss Mary." I liked her from the first minute because she patted my head and asked me to sit next to her on a small bench and share the tea cakes. After we had visited for a while and eaten two or three tea cakes, she invited me to help her water her plants. She showed me how to hold the sprinkling can, and as I followed her about her garden she said, "Isn't Easter Sunday a wonderful day?"

I said I thought it was too. After all, I was wearing a brand new pink dotted Swiss dress. But when she spoke again, I knew she wasn't thinking about my pretty new clothes. "God is love," she said. "God loves you a lot, child. He loves you more than you can imagine." Even though I knew about God's love, or thought I did because we heard about him every week in Sunday school, I didn't understand what she said next: "Just think, today we are celebrating the Resurrection of Jesus. Did you know it happened in a garden? Maybe a flower garden like mine?"

I wanted to say yes because I wanted Miss Mary for my friend and I didn't want her to think I was ignorant. On the other hand, if I pretended to know something that I didn't, she might ask me about it and then I would feel awful. So I said, "My Sunday school teacher told us about Jesus, but what does Resurrection mean? She didn't tell us that."

For a moment she stood there looking thoughtful. Then she took off her hat and said, "Come with me."

She took my hand, and we walked to a part of the yard I had not seen before. She led me to a vine-covered bower that cradled a small swing. "Let's sit here and talk," she said.

The swing moved ever so gently back and forth with my feet hanging over the edge, unable to reach the ground. As we sat close together, she told me about Easter.

"When Jesus died on the cross," she explained, "some of His friends buried Him. Three days later He came alive again. He was resurrected from the dead. That's what the big word means. And that's what happened on Easter, the first Easter. Yes, Jesus died and came back to life to show the world that we too will never die, but have everlasting life. That means you and me. And today Jesus still lives. He is with us now. Right here in this garden."

I looked around quickly, but I didn't see anyone. I wondered how Miss Mary could see Jesus and I couldn't. But because she said He was there, I believed her. And because I wanted so much for her to be my friend, I found myself wanting to see Him, wanting to know He was there, wanting to feel His presence. Now, many years afterward, I count that as the moment my Christian faith was born.

Throughout our lifelong friendship that began in her garden, I did learn to feel His presence. I came to know that He is near me wherever I go; in the kitchen as I prepare dinner, beside me as I interview guests on my television show, and even now as I sit at my typewriter telling this story. But nowhere have I ever felt His presence more strongly than in Miss Mary's garden.

My new neighbor quickly became my dearest friend. As a first grader, my school day was over early, and I could hardly wait to rush home and then go next door to visit. As I try to recall those days, I seem to remember that Miss Mary had a hand in teaching me to read and write. Of course, any story about Miss Mary must include a mention of her signs, made from the tops of wooden cigar boxes. To this day I remember some of them. One said, "Watch out! Low-flying butterflies." And one, which she put in the zinnia bed: "B-careful, B's at work."

One little sign—decorated with colorful flowers and birds—I couldn't read. I didn't know what its poem said. And by the time I could read a poem or two, the hedge had grown over it and I had forgotten about it.

During those afternoons together, Miss Mary taught me how to prepare seedbeds, how to sprinkle fertilizer where it was needed, how to spray plants for insects and how to weed the flowerbeds.

She taught me other things too, more important things. She taught me how to pray. Oh, I knew how to say my prayers before I went to sleep at night. And I could repeat the Lord's Prayer pretty well. But Miss Mary taught me how to communicate with God. "The Bible tells us to pray without ceasing," she said. And she did. The first few times I heard her, I thought she was just talking to herself until I discovered she was praying.

Miss Mary not only talked to God about her problems, she talked to Him about mine. When I would tell her about some first- or second- or third-grade crisis, she would say, "Let's talk to Jesus about it." Then she would stop her work and we would go to the swing and pray together.

Then we moved away. Although I didn't see Miss Mary every day, I did try to visit her from time to time. As I became a teenager and later a student at the university and later after I married, I saw less and less of her.

Then one day her nephew telephoned to say Miss Mary had died peacefully. There is no way to express my grief. Just let me say that I suffered through all of the anguish that comes when you lose your best friend.

On the day of her funeral, I stood teary-eyed following the final graveside prayer. Quietly her nephew asked me, "Would you like to stop by her house while you are nearby? We must sell it, and I know how much you enjoyed her garden. Maybe you would like to visit it one more time and see how well she kept it up, even to the last."

"Oh yes," and even as I said it, my tears stopped and my sadness waned a bit. "Oh, how thoughtful of you," I said. "Maybe right now?"

My husband Dexter drove the car. As he stopped near Miss Mary's driveway, he said, "Take your time. I'll wait here."

The moment I stepped into the garden, my tears ceased and the ache in my heart melted. I began to relive my first visit on that Easter Sunday so long ago. There was Miss Mary, smiling at me. She was wearing her old straw hat, her watering can in her hand. Oh, I couldn't see her, of course, but I felt her presence, just as she had taught me to feel the presence of Jesus.

"Come, hurry," she seemed to say. I knew exactly what she meant, and I rushed toward our favorite place, the swing in the vine-covered bower. There it hung, needing a coat of paint, but still our swing. I sat in it and made it move back and forth. I heard Miss Mary say, "Jesus lives. He died and came back from the dead. He overcame death to show us that we, too, will never die but will have eternal life. That means you and me. He is with us now."

Suddenly, like the sun coming from behind a cloud, the full meaning of our first conversation became clear. I did understand, at last. Then, sitting there, I heard again the words of one of my favorite hymns, "He lives! He lives! Christ Jesus lives today." And I knew that just as surely, Miss Mary lives.

A squirrel chattered at me from a nearby tree and reminded me that Dexter was waiting. I stood up because there was no longer a need to reflect. I had found what I had been searching for—the joy that comes with understanding. So, with my tears completely gone, I wound my way through Miss Mary's garden for the last time.

When I turned the corner and headed toward the driveway, I realized that the old hedge had been removed and in its place a bed of pansy faces smiled at me. And there in the midst was that little sign, which I had not been able to read when I was a first grader. Most of the paint had peeled and the words were dim. But I still was able to make them out. This is what I read:

> The kiss of sun for pardon,
> The song of the birds for mirth—
> One is nearer God's heart in a garden
> Than anywhere else on earth.
> —Dorothy Frances Gurney

TRAVELING COMPANION

by Karen Rego

My four-year-old son Wil endured terrible leg pains. After consulting various doctors, my husband Tom and I were told Wil was probably suffering from arthralgia—difficult growing pains. We learned to live with his complaints and help him bear the pain. But one of the hardest times we had was during a trip to Florida.

We were flying to Miami to attend a wedding. Wil and his seven-year-old brother Matthew sat in window seats so they could enjoy their first jet ride. Suddenly I heard Wil say to his daddy, "My leg hurts."

I rubbed Wil's leg constantly, but his cries grew until they echoed throughout the cabin. I had never felt so helpless. God, be with us, I prayed. Finally we landed and Wil made his way uneasily out of the plane.

The following day Wil was fine. We enjoyed the wedding and a few days of vacation, then boarded the plane for our flight home. We were in the air less than five minutes when, to my relief, Wil fell asleep. He slept through the entire flight.

The next Sunday was Palm Sunday. During our service, in a reenactment of Christ's entry into Jerusalem, a member of our congregation dressed as Jesus came down the aisle. Wil turned to his daddy and asked, "Is that the real Jesus?"

"No," Tom replied, "Jesus is up in heaven."

Wil nodded. "Like on the jet?"

Startled, I asked him to repeat what he had said. "The real Jesus," he replied, "was next to me on that big jet."

"You saw someone on the plane who looked like Jesus?" I asked.

"No," Wil replied matter-of-factly. "I saw Jesus. Outside my window.

"I told Jesus my leg was hurting," he continued, "and he said, 'No problem. I'll take care of you.' Then I told Jesus I'd take care of him too." I asked Wil if he was speaking of the flight returning from Florida. Wil said, "Mama, you know my legs weren't hurting on the way home."

After church Wil repeated his story as if it had been an everyday occurrence. "Next time I want you and Daddy to look out the window so you can see Jesus too," Wil said, and then added, "I wasn't even looking for him. He was just there."

Once we had landed in Miami and the time of hardship was over, Jesus simply, in Wil's words, "floated away." My son's experience reminded me that whether we can see Jesus or not, we remain in his loving embrace always.

WAS JESUS DISAPPOINTED?

by Carol Kuykendall

Jesus must have felt desperately lonely and in need of loyal friends the night He led his eleven disciples into the Garden of Gethsemane after their Passover meal. He left eight disciples at the entrance, telling them, "Sit here, while I go yonder and pray." But He asked three of them, Peter, James and John, to accompany Him deeper into the garden. "My soul is very sorrowful, even to death," he told them. "Remain here, and watch with me" (Matthew 26:36, 38 RSV). Then He moved away to a secluded spot and fell on His knees to pray.

Soon He returned to His three trusted disciples and found them asleep. He awakened Peter and asked him, "Could you not watch with me one hour?" Again He retreated to pray alone, and again He returned to find the disciples asleep. The scene repeated itself a third and final time.

Was Jesus disappointed in these close friends? I remember a day not long ago when I wandered around our silent home aching with loneliness, longing for the phone to ring, to hear the voice of a perfect friend who had the perfect words to fill the emptiness I felt. The phone didn't ring, and finally, I sat down to talk to Jesus, realizing that no other friend would ever fill that longing because all human relationships have imperfections.

As much as I love my family and friends, each may disappoint me or fall short at some time. Only Jesus gives me perfect, consistent and complete love. And He's the One I can count on. Always.

Still all my song shall be,
nearer, my God to thee.

—SARAH ADAMS

THIS CYCLE OF FEAR

by Pat Mofford

It was the kind of quiet afternoon at home that I love. I was polishing furniture and letting my thoughts wander when a question popped into my head that I knew my teenage daughter could answer.

I went upstairs and, as I'd guessed, Becky was in my room lying on the bed and talking on the phone. I stepped through the doorway and started to speak, when suddenly my mind seemed to leave my body. I opened my mouth, but no words came out.

Becky's eyes went wide. She hung up quickly. "Mom! What's wrong?"

After a long moment, I gasped, "I . . . feel so strange. . . . I can't think."

Becky knew I was nervous. Her father was away on a work assignment in Alaska. "Mom, you'll be okay," she said.

I nodded and hurried downstairs, afraid to say aloud what I was feeling. What's happening to me? I'd had panic attacks before, but never like this. I had managed to keep them a secret from our two children and from Curt too. In the early years of our marriage I'd suffered from depression and had even attempted suicide. Ever since my treatment, I'd been taking medication. My doctor explained I'd need it for the rest of my life because my depression resulted from a chemical imbalance.

I didn't ever again want to put Curt or our children through the suffering of having a wife and mother who was that ill. When we went out together, I never let on that walking arm in arm with Curt or holding his hand helped me fight off panic attacks. For his part, Curt seemed to understand and accept whatever excuse I gave if I said I didn't feel like going out.

After that terrifying moment upstairs with Becky, I calmed down and felt all right the rest of the day. *Maybe I will get better,* I told myself. After all, I had always been able to fend off previous panic attacks.

But as the weeks went by with Curt still in Fairbanks, I suffered more attacks and began to withdraw. It took all my willpower to go out to buy groceries. I kept the drapes closed. I felt threatened by everything that went on outside my house. When a friend came to take me shopping, once again I felt my mind leave my body. All I could think was: *Am I dying? Is this how it feels?*

At last Curt returned. But I was still fearful constantly. In desperation I called my doctor. He gave me a second medication.

One evening Curt came in from work with a big smile. "I stopped by the folks' house," he said excitedly. "They want us to go with them to the World's Fair in British Columbia. We can camp in the van."

"Oh, Curt, I can't!" I exclaimed, shaking my head. "I really don't want to go."

A look of disappointment crossed his face, but he said, "Okay. I guess we'll go without you."

I retreated to the kitchen to finish preparing supper. So often Curt had to go places alone when I should have been with him—auto races, fairs, bowling—all the things couples do for fun. I was failing him.

Yet how could I tell him that some days I was utterly terrified in my own home—that the prospect of driving for hours to a strange place filled me with dread? How could he—how could anyone—understand the overwhelming fear I sometimes felt?

I gazed at the familiar surroundings in my kitchen. It had always been a refuge for me, but now I felt as if I'd become prisoner. *Oh, Lord,* I prayed, *how can I break this cycle of fear? I feel like·I'm being strangled. Please help me!*

In the quiet moment after my frantic plea, it seemed as if God said, *Go. I will be with you. You only have to take one step at a time.*

Curt wandered into the kitchen. I turned to him and said, "I think I was a little hasty in my decision. I want to go to the fair with you."

Being a man of few words, he walked over, wrapped his arms around me and gave me a big hug.

While we planned and packed, I prayed a lot. Becky and our son Kent wanted to stay home. Curt and I would sleep in the van on foam pads and eat our meals with his folks in their RV. When it was time to go, I climbed into the van, praying, *Lord, here we go. I know You are with me.* During the six-hour drive north to Vancouver, British Columbia, I reminded myself constantly that God was with me.

The morning after we arrived, we drove to the fair, parked the van and started to walk toward the exposition area. The wide entrance loomed menacingly before me; hundreds of people swarmed the fairground. There were bright flags everywhere snapping in the breeze. My eyes darted from one flag to the next. Strange aromas of exotic foods were thick in the air. I began to have trouble catching my breath. People's voices, some in languages I'd never heard before, were roaring in my ears.

I started to blank out. I stopped in my tracks, paralyzed with fear.

Curt's worried eyes searched mine. "Pat," he asked softly, "is something wrong?"

"I'll be all right," I managed to stammer. "I just need to rest a minute." Desperate for assurance, I imagined Jesus standing beside me. I pictured His kind, calm face next to mine, His cool hand gently holding mine. With Curt physically on one side of me and Jesus on the other in spirit, my head began to clear. My breathing became normal.

Here we go, Lord. I willed my foot to take the first step. And another.

We moved into the crowd at the entrance. I continued to imagine Jesus standing between me and all harm. Now the spectacle had changed; the flags waved gaily, welcomingly, and the scent of spicy food was enticing.

Curt pointed out the Chinese building. "Let's go in there!"

There was a long line waiting to get inside. Standing in line always gave me claustrophobia. But Curt was already leading me over. I noticed a lady knitting to pass time. I prayed, *Oh, Lord, keep holding my hand.*

My heart stayed calm. I even started a conversation with the lady who was knitting, and soon we were inside, gazing at beautiful tapestries, vases and glassware. An artisan was creating a picture of a cat out of strands of silk thread. It was gorgeous. Another she'd completed was for sale. "Oh, Curt, look! Only a thousand dollars," I teased. He laughed, knowing I loved cats enough to have bought it—if I had had the money.

After that we entered an enormous building. My heart lurched. I wanted to run out. No. Jesus is right here with me. I fixed my mind on Him and followed the tug of Curt's hand.

All that day and the next I toured the fair with Curt and his family. I did not have another panic attack.

After we returned home, I felt rested—even exhilarated. I had taken a giant step! So I began to set goals to overcome all the fears that had nagged me earlier. Little steps, like a trip to the mall, became much easier for me.

Now on every outing I say, "Here I am again, Lord." And off we go, hand in hand.

A FRIEND IN NEED

by Marilyn Morgan King

Tired of lying in bed counting the ceiling tiles in the closed-up bedroom, I forced myself to get up, open the drapes and brush my teeth. Then I fell back into bed, exhausted. A fine way to start another Monday, I thought. Would I ever get over this energy-sapping virus? The fever and sore throat, the aching muscles and pounding headache were finally gone, but I couldn't seem to get back my strength.

And there was something else: a dull, hollow ache right in the center of my chest, a deep inner yearning so intense it felt almost physical. What was causing this empty feeling? Surely not loneliness! I had a loving husband, children and grandchildren, some very dear friends, people around me most of the time. In fact, I'd always treasured my time alone, never feeling I got quite enough of it.

No, I was sure it couldn't be loneliness. I knew how that felt. Looking out the bedroom window at the dull gray autumn sky, I recalled my junior high semester in Chicago during World War II while my father was in the Navy. I just hadn't fit in with the teenagers there as I had back home in McCook, Nebraska. My clothes weren't right. I didn't talk the way they did. I didn't know their games. I spent a lot of time alone.

Yet looking back on those Chicago days, I saw that I had developed a very precious friendship during that lonely time. Every night, I complained to my friend about feeling left out. In the mornings, we walked to school together. Often during recess, he and I would sit together, leaning against the brick building, and talk about the little triumphs of the day (a good grade on a test, an encouraging word from a teacher). We also talked about the hurtful moments of being left out of games or feeling whispered about. My friend's name was Jesus.

Lying in bed now, I realized I hadn't felt that kind of easy comradeship with Christ for a long time. When had that personal closeness, the comfortable intimacy with my friend disappeared? Maybe it was during my years as a young mother. The ache had come back then, but not for long, because I quickly discovered a new way to escape it. Some people reach for alcohol or drugs to numb the pain. Some overeat or bury themselves in their work. For a while social activities became my painkiller—bridge clubs, luncheons, coffees, teas, meetings. Then one afternoon at a bridge party, I found myself asking, "Why am I doing this?" And I didn't have an answer.

So I gave up all of that social hoopla and went back to college to get my master's degree. Again the ache went away. What a relief! I kept busy with my family, schoolwork and, later, teaching and writing—busy enough that I wasn't aware of any inner emptiness for, well, maybe twenty years.

Now here I was with this silly virus that was lasting too long. Because it was denying me my usual painkillers (work, speaking engagements, playing with my grandchildren, busying myself around the house), I was feeling that old ache again. Could it be that it had never really left, but had merely been pushed down and covered over?

My husband came home at noon and fixed me a bowl of soup, but I ate only a few spoonfuls. After he left to go back to work, I tossed and turned for an hour or so and then, out of boredom and despair, propped myself up in bed and reached for my Bible. I didn't really expect Bible reading to ease the inner longing, but it was about the only thing I seemed able to do at that point.

Once I started, I read for many hours each day, and I discovered something that left me absolutely stunned: Every major figure—from Abraham to Jacob to David to the prophets to Jesus to the disciples to Paul—had experienced the same lonely ache I was feeling! Really! I wondered, *Could it be that everyone has an empty place within, even those of us who try to deny it or numb it or run away from it? Was it possible that God Himself had put it there, hoping we'd fill it with Him?*

From somewhere outside I heard the whack of a ball against a bat, children cheering, a dog barking. And in the flash of that moment, I knew it was true. I also knew that nothing less than God Himself could satisfy this deep-inside longing.

Eagerly I began to reread some of those Bible stories to find out how the fathers of our faith had handled their loneliness. In Genesis I read that when God told Abraham to leave his country, his kindred and his father's house, he did it. How lonely he must have been! We are told that "a dread and great darkness fell upon him" (Genesis 15:12 RSV).

So what did Abraham do? One thing he most certainly did not do was to run away from his pain! Instead he talked to God the way I had talked to my friend Jesus during those lonely Chicago years. He complained about the things that were going wrong in his life. He argued with God. He laid his anger before the Lord. He even admitted his doubts to God. Abraham handled his loneliness by being absolutely real and completely honest with God. I wondered if I could do that.

I closed my Bible, placed it on the bedside table and looked at the clock. It was 3:30 AM. My husband wouldn't be home for another hour. Even though it felt a little strange at first, I began speaking aloud to God. I told Him I was sick and tired of being sick. "Besides that, I'm scared. What if there's something more serious wrong with me? What if I've got cancer or something?" Somehow, just voicing that fear aloud took away a little of its terror. Then I poured out some anger I'd been feeling about an unfair situation in another area of my life. "Look, Lord, I've been praying for a resolution to this problem for a year and a half, and it doesn't seem to be getting one bit better! And I'm mad at You about that!"

Oh! I couldn't believe I'd really said that. But the feelings were honest, and they came from deep inside me, where the ache was. Almost as soon as the words were out of my mouth, I felt pounds lighter; it was as if I'd fallen, limp and spent, into unconditionally loving arms.

Tuesday morning, for the first time since the virus hit, I had toast and coffee in the kitchen instead of the bedroom. Then I turned to the Psalms. Who could have been more lonely than David, whose friends deserted him, whose own son turned against him, whose soul thirsted for God "as in a dry and weary land where no water is" (Psalm 63:1 RSV)? Oh, those words hit me right where the ache was. But then I saw that instead of trying to run away from his desert of the heart, David had written out his feelings, both the negative and the positive ones, just as they came to him. "How long, O Lord? Wilt thou forget me for ever? . . . How long must I bear pain in my soul, and have sorrow in my heart all the day?" But just a few lines later, "I have trusted in thy steadfast love; my heart shall rejoice in thy salvation" (Psalm 13:1–2, 5 RSV).

I got out my spiral-bound notebook and began writing. Pain and praise, grief and thanksgiving, fear and hope spilled alternately onto the pages. Then, like the Israelites, I spoke aloud some of what I'd written. What a great physical, emotional and spiritual release! By the time I'd finished, both my heart and my voice were singing.

By Wednesday I was feeling much better physically, but the lonely ache was not completely gone. It wasn't heavy anymore, but it just sat there near my heart, gnawing. Maybe I could learn something about coping with loneliness from Jesus. I turned to the 22nd chapter of Luke. No one could have been more alone than our Lord was that night in the Garden of Gethsemane. While He prayed, knowing that death awaited Him, His trusted disciples abandoned Him by falling asleep. How honest was His cry to God! "Father, if thou art willing, remove this cup from me." Oh, I felt so close to Jesus as I thought of Him in that hour of utter loneliness. It made me realize that He knew what I was feeling this very moment! Jesus faced His darkness by saying, "Nevertheless not my will, but thine, be done" (v. 42 RSV). As soon as He'd said that, an angel had come and strengthened Him.

I knelt down by the bed and named all the areas of my life that I'd been trying so hard to control. "My children's futures, Lord—they're Yours, not mine." A career decision. "You decide, God." My health. "Not my will but Yours." One by one I named my concerns and relinquished them to my heavenly Father. I didn't see an angel, but as soon as I'd finished my prayer, it seemed to me that something happened that eased the ache.

By Thursday I felt well enough to get dressed and do a bit of housework. After lunch I sat down with my Bible and picked up where I'd left off, in Luke's Gospel. What a sense of desolation and abandonment the apostles must have felt after the man they'd invested every ounce of their faith in had died and been buried! On the road to Emmaus I shared the loneliness of those two disciples whose Master had been crucified. What joy it must have been for them to discover, later, that the stranger who walked with them was none other than their precious friend Jesus! Their loneliness had been broken as He walked with them.

I looked out my kitchen window. It was a golden autumn day. If I went out for a walk, would Jesus come and walk with me as He had done with the disciples? I put on my old blue windbreaker and started down the sidewalk. Oh, how good it felt to be outside, after all those weeks. As I walked, I listened deep inside until I could hear Jesus' words: "Lo, I am with you always, to the close of the age" (Matthew 28:20 RSV).

I said His words over and over in my mind as I walked, and by the time I got to Lakeview Drive, a great healing warmth had come into my chest near my heart. As I continued to walk, I began to feel a quiet, gentle Presence near me. Everything I saw and heard seemed to enter into the very core of me—the song of the birds, the swish and sway of the tall grass, the scent of wet leaves. I wanted to shout, raise my hands to God, dance! Of course, I'm far too inhibited to do that where people might see me, but I did feel a bounce in my step, a lilt in my body movements. It was very much like being in love. I was happy to the edge of tears—and no longer alone.

When I got home, I knelt down and thanked God for Abraham and David and Jesus and the disciples and all of the other Bible greats who had taught me that we all live with an ache of loneliness. I knew that my own ache would come back again sometime. But I also knew that when it did, I'd use it to develop closer companionship with Christ. And that thought filled every empty place inside me.

There is a friend
who sticks closer than a brother.

—PROVERBS 18:24 (NIV)

MOVING NEARER TO THE CIRCLE

by Sue Monk Kidd

When we were eleven years old, my friend Connie and I went to a very "outback" Girl Scout camp. Upon arriving we found that we had been assigned to a wonderful counselor named Robbie. But we soon discovered that we'd been assigned chores too—peeling potatoes, scrubbing cabin floors, and cleaning latrines. Even on our pleasure hikes we were constantly enlisted to gather firewood, clear away rocks or carry equipment.

We noticed that the girls closest to Robbie always had the greatest number of chores to do. It seemed that whoever was the nearest at hand was volunteered. Therefore, on future hikes we developed the artful strategy of walking at a safe distance. We didn't fall so far back that we might become lost, but neither did we stay so close that we might become involved in any hard work. Staying at a safe distance took a lot of finesse, but we pulled it off for about a week, escaping all sorts of tasks.

Then one sunny afternoon we saw the other girls sitting in a circle under the boughs of a big, spreading tree—laughing and, we imagined, sharing delicious secrets with Robbie, who sat in their midst. We stood to one side by ourselves and watched. We felt apart, excluded, alone. That's when it dawned on us that we had also escaped the joy of forming a close and happy friendship with our counselor. So we moved nearer to the circle, and soon we were once again hauling firewood. But in closing ranks with our counselor, we made our last week at camp a truly rewarding experience.

I think that the closer we stay to Christ, the deeper is our awareness of the Gospels' true demands. But only when we stand back, we find that we are alone, out of His circle. It's His friendship that makes life abundant and enriching.

We have only to stay close.

· PART 2 ·

Glimpses of Jesus
as Savior and Lord

IN BOTH OF THE GOSPEL ACCOUNTS OF JESUS' BIRTH, an angel states the name of the unborn child and then foretells His mission. In Matthew 1:21 (NIV) an angel speaks to Joseph: ". . . you are to give him the name Jesus, because he will save his people from their sins." In Luke 1:31, 33 (NIV) Gabriel addresses Mary, with a different emphasis: ". . . you are to give him the name Jesus. . . . his kingdom will never end." These two aspects, Savior and Lord, become the critical message of the angel's birth announcement to the shepherds: "Today . . . a Savior has been born to you; he is Christ the Lord" (Luke 2:11 NIV).

The stories in this section give me a deeper understanding of Jesus' role as Savior and Lord on a very personal level. I think of an old gospel song by Fanny Crosby, "A Wonderful Savior Is Jesus My Lord." And also on a grander scale, dramatically portrayed in a woman's "Vision of Glory" on the horizon of the Atlantic Ocean.

May these glimpses of Jesus draw you closer to Him, in faith.

THE JESUS RESCUE

by Marion Bond West

When I was quite young, my mother and I lived with three other families in a long, brown-shingled apartment house with green awnings. That Christmas we watched with fascination as I. V. Hulme, who lived in one of the apartments, erected a huge nativity scene in the front yard. Even though it was cold enough to see my breath, I stayed outside and watched all the activity—hammering, measuring, sawing. The manger was flat like a billboard and the figures were two-dimensional cutouts. But it looked magnificent to me. The story of Christmas—Baby Jesus—had come to my front yard.

At night the scene was illuminated by hidden lights, and the pointed star high above looked absolutely real. During the day, I'd go up close to the scene. Somehow, I felt like an actual part of it, as though I too had come to worship the Christ Child. "Hi, Baby Jesus," I'd say, "I'm glad You're in my front yard this Christmas." On Christmas morning, I bundled up and ran outside to see Him even before I'd opened my presents. I gave Him a kiss and whispered, "Happy birthday, Jesus!" I longed to "rescue" the Baby and take Him inside where it was warm.

I had no idea it was He who had come to rescue me.

AN ODD LITTLE MAN

by Diana J. Jeansonne

Mr. Morgan was sad and frail looking, with eyes that appeared to hold a painful secret. To my junior-high scrutiny, he seemed an odd little man, pale and sickly. He was our new Sunday-school teacher, and during that first class I thought: *I am never coming back here.* He wasn't fun or entertaining, and his teaching style was not peppy enough for my taste.

To add to the boredom, Mr. Morgan wanted to close the lesson not in prayer, as we always did, but in song. I couldn't wait to get out of there as we started to sing the first stanza of "The Old Rugged Cross."

> On a hill far away, stood an old rugged cross,
> the emblem of suffering and shame . . .

Suddenly a noise made me look up. It was a sniffle. A tear trickled down Mr. Morgan's cheek.

> And I love that old cross,
> where the dearest and best
> for a world of lost sinners was slain.

There was another tear, and another. *What is this poor man so upset about?* I wondered.

So I'll cherish the old rugged cross . . .

He seemed to be trying to hold back his tears, but they continued despite his best efforts. At first, the boys looked embarrassed. Then they began snickering, elbow-jabbing and pointing. The girls found it too painful even to look up; their eyes remained glued to the pages in front of them.

But I had never seen a man cry. I couldn't take my eyes off the teacher.

I will cling to the old rugged cross
and exchange it some day for a crown.

The song ended, and Mr. Morgan blew his nose on a handkerchief. "I'm sorry," he said. "I just can't sing that hymn without thinking of what Jesus did for me. He hung there, almost naked, on a rough wooden cross. A spear was stuck in His side and He spilled His blood. For what? For me! For my sins."

All the sniggers had stopped. There was complete silence in the classroom now. Everyone was still as Mr. Morgan paused and looked around at us.

"And for your sins too," he said. "Because of Him, we have a home in heaven forever."

I was overwhelmed and in awe. I had never heard a man make such a personal, down-to-earth statement about salvation before. Even to the mind of a seventh grader, the meaning was apparent: Mr. Morgan made it clear that Christ was his reason for living. The tears he shed were tears of gratitude. And through them, for the first time, I saw a personal God. Until that moment, Jesus had been merely a character in a book. I had never before been grateful for—and to—Christ.

I haven't forgotten that day thirty years ago or Mr. Morgan's gift. He taught me that there is no greater joy than throwing your pride, and a few shed tears, to the wind, if hearts are implanted with the seeds that open eternity.

THE SERVICE I DIDN'T WANT TO ATTEND

by Betty Graham

At the end of our Maundy Thursday potluck supper, our pastor blessed a loaf of bread and broke it into pieces, passing it and the wine down the long tables, inviting all to partake. "This is the way it must have been at the Last Supper," he said. It felt right, it felt good—another special occasion at the church whose services I'd loved and participated in for years.

When the pastor said he hoped to see us all at the Good Friday service the following night, I nodded. Of course I'd be there.

"But this year," the pastor was saying, "we'll be doing something different. You all know the large wooden cross that we cover with flowers and place in the front of the sanctuary on Easter Sunday . . ."

I was thrilled just thinking of it, that beautiful flower-covered cross, the glorious symbol of Christ's Resurrection.

"This year at the end of our Good Friday service, that bare cross will be placed at the back of the sanctuary. At the close of the service, you will each receive a nail to put into the cross where Christ's hands or feet would have been. It will remind us that He was crucified for our sins."

In an instant the mood of the evening was shattered for me. This didn't feel right at all. *No! I could never put a nail into that wood!* I shuddered. For all our pastor's other excellent ideas, this one was chilling, off the mark.

As I drove home, my mind was racing. It had been such a beautiful spring day—daffodils in the churchyard, tulip trees and forsythia and japonica in full bloom. Why did the pastor have to spoil it now?

I got ready for bed, thinking more and more about the Good Friday service. I wouldn't go—couldn't go. I wasn't responsible for Christ's suffering, I wasn't among His executioners. Nor would I ever be, even symbolically. All my life I've been active in church, have tried to do my best to follow Christ's teachings. I know that the Crucifixion was horrible, but my thoughts had always rushed on to the events of Easter morning: Christ's Resurrection. That brought joy.

I tossed and turned most of the night, and when I finally dozed off, my dreams tormented me. I saw myself at the foot of the cross on Golgotha, hammer in hand, ready to drive a spike into our Lord's flesh. My head was bowed, I could not look up into His eyes. The weight of the hammer seemed to pull my arm from its socket. The Roman soldiers joked and laughed in the background, and the gray sky rumbled like a moan.

And then Christ spoke, as if directly to me. ". . . inasmuch as you did it to one of the least of these My brethren, you did it to Me" (Matthew 25:40 NKJV).

"But I didn't!" I shouted. "I'm not a violent person. I don't go around hurting people."

I don't know if I cried out, but when I awoke I was shaking. My hands were clenched and clammy. Just then the alarm went off and I was back in the everyday world. Thank goodness, it was only a dream.

I dressed for work and started my long commute. Normally I don't remember my dreams at all. But this one was so powerful that I played it again and again in my mind. As I pulled into the parking lot of the publications office where I work, I realized that I'd been so preoccupied I didn't remember driving those thirty-five miles.

I was in the ladies' room staring into the mirror and thinking about all of this when another woman walked in, a woman I didn't like very much. She had a look on her face that I interpreted as a scowl, and I'd avoided her whenever possible. I nodded at her, secretly resentful that she worked here.

And then as I looked into the mirror, it hit me. What had I said this morning? That I didn't go around hurting people? And yet wasn't I hurting her by judging her, criticizing her? No matter how unlovable she seemed to me, God loved her no matter what.

Inasmuch as you did it to one of the least of these . . .

Driving home in the pouring rain, I thought of the many ways that every day, day after day, I do hurt Christ—in a sharp response, a bit of careless gossip, a flash of anger when things haven't gone my way, impatience with my children, a snap judgment about someone before I know the facts. Each item seemed like another nail adding to the pain of the figure on the cross.

You did it to Me.

Was this the message I was supposed to hear? Was this Christ's way of reminding me that I too cause Him pain every time I act without love or understanding?

So I went to the Good Friday service after all. Sitting in the darkened sanctuary, I prayed for forgiveness more sincerely than ever before. As I received the sacraments at the altar, I thanked Him for giving us in the rite of Communion a chance to begin again.

When the service ended, I filed out with the others to the huge cross in the narthex and received two nails from the usher.

It was not a comfortable feeling to place a nail in one of the holes where Christ's hand would have been, but reverently I put it there. The other nail I put in my purse as our pastor had instructed. I carry it with me every day, lest I forget again.

HE BOUGHT US BACK

by Drue Duke

On top of a chest in our den is displayed proudly a hand-carved sailboat that my husband made as a boy. It reminds me of a story I once heard of another little boy who also carved a boat. He delighted in sailing it in the river near his home. One day the boat was caught up in the current and swept out of sight. The boy asked his father to help him search, but they could not find it.

Several months later, while visiting in a town downstream, the boy saw his boat for sale in a store window. Excitedly, he rushed to his father and got the money to purchase it. When he held it in his arms at last, he told the storekeeper, "Now it is twice mine. Once because I made it and again because I bought it back."

We are twice God's. First because He made us and again because, through Jesus Christ, He bought us back.

THE DRAGON AND THE PREACHER

by Johnny Lee Clary

I first met Reverend Wade Watts when we both were asked to speak on a
Tulsa radio program. He put out his hand and I stepped back, offended.
I was the Grand Dragon of the Ku Klux Klan in Oklahoma and he was
the state president of the NAACP. There was no way you would catch me
shaking hands with him.

My training in hate began early. I was five years old when my father
encouraged me to lean out our car window and shout racial slurs as we
passed a bus stop. Daddy grinned and patted me on the back. "That's my
boy," he said. When I was older I sat up late at night listening to stories
my Uncle Harold told about shooting at black men who crossed his property. Daddy and Uncle Harold would howl with laughter.

My grandmother, though, read to me from the Bible and prayed for
me. Once I came home from Sunday school singing a song I had learned:
"Jesus loves the little children, All the children of the world; Red and yellow, black and white, They are precious in His sight . . ."

"Don't ever let me catch you singing words like that again!" Daddy's
voice thundered. That was the end of Sunday school for me.

One night when I was eleven, I came home and found Daddy standing with a gun to his head. As I watched in horror, he pulled the trigger.

After the funeral, Mama sent me to California to live with my older sister and her boyfriend. Lonely and confused, I spent a lot of time staring at the TV, and one day I saw a talk-show host interviewing David Duke, the Grand Wizard of the Ku Klux Klan. Fascinated, I asked around about how to get in touch with the Klan, and before long a representative came to visit. "Son," he said, "what you need is a real family—the Klan."

Week after week he showed up to take me to meetings. Desperate to belong to something, at the age of fourteen I joined as a full-fledged member. Eventually I became David Duke's bodyguard, and by the time I was twenty I had become the Grand Dragon of Oklahoma.

I was a tireless recruiter for the Klan in Oklahoma, and it grew under my leadership. I was a fiery speaker, spreading the gospel of hate. That's why when I was asked to speak at that particular radio station in Tulsa in 1979, I jumped at the chance. Only shortly before the program did I learn it would be a debate between the NAACP's Reverend Wade Watts and me. But I wasn't worried. I looked forward to it—a chance to put a black man in his place.

So I refused to shake hands with the nicely dressed older gentleman carrying a worn Bible. But as I took in his strong, kind face and dignified manner, he reached out and shook my hand anyway. "Hello, Mr. Clary," he said. "I'm Reverend Watts. Before we go in, I just want you to know that I love you and Jesus loves you."

Our on-air debate went back and forth, me firing off reasons the races should never have anything to do with each other, and the Reverend politely refuting everything I said and quoting Scripture. When he zeroed in on me with pointed questions about the beliefs I held, I could only mumble the generic slogans of the Klan. I became flustered by his calm. "I'm not listening to any more," I snarled, storming out.

I gathered my things and was heading through the lobby when the Reverend appeared. I would have gladly pushed him out of my way except that he was holding a baby in his arms. "Mr. Clary, this is my daughter Tia," he said. "And I have one last question for you." He held out a little girl with shining dark eyes and skin, and one of the sweetest expressions I had ever seen. "You say you hate all black people, Mr. Clary. Just tell me—how can you hate this child?"

Stunned, I turned and almost ran. I heard the Reverend call after me: "I'm going to love you and pray for you, Mr. Clary, whether you like it or not!"

I didn't like it. Over the next ten years I had two burning goals. One was to climb the Klan's national ranks to the position of Imperial Wizard. The second was to make Reverend Wade Watts pay for what he had done. I would make him hate me.

But as ferociously as the Oklahoma Klan continued its campaign, just as firmly Reverend Wade Watts worked for justice and equality. Klansmen barraged his family with threatening phone calls. His windows were broken; effigies were torched on his lawn. His church was burned to the ground. The thirteen Watts children—a number of whom were adopted—were threatened and had to be escorted to school by the highway patrol. Once or twice I found myself thinking about that baby, little Tia. I drove the thought away with hate. Still, nothing the Klan did stopped the Reverend, nothing shut him up. When he joined ranks with an Oklahoma senator to outlaw the telephone hotlines we used for recruiting, we called an emergency meeting. Klan members crowded around me as I dialed the Watts home.

"I want you to know we're coming to get you," I hissed when the Reverend answered. "And this time we mean business . . ."

"Hello, Johnny Lee!" he said, as though hearing from a long-lost relative. "You don't have to come for me, I'll meet you. How about at a nice little restaurant I know out on Highway 270? I'm buying."

"This isn't a joke, old man. We're coming over, and when we're finished, you'll wish you'd never crossed us."

"This place has the best home cooking you ever tasted. Apple pie that'll make you long for more. Fluffy mashed potatoes. Iced tea in mason jars . . . . "

I slammed down the phone. "He wants to take us out to dinner," I said in disbelief. "Talked about apple pie and iced tea."

"The old man's gone crazy," someone said. "Let's forget about him."

We left Reverend Wade Watts alone after that. I turned my energies to solidifying my position in my "family," and in 1989 I was appointed Imperial Wizard. I had just gone through a divorce and lost custody of my baby daughter, and in desperation I focused on a new goal. I wanted to unify all hate groups—from skinheads to neo-Nazis—under the umbrella of the Klan. I arranged a national meeting where those groups would convene and, I hoped, unite in strength.

That was to be the culmination of my efforts. But on the day of the gathering, the Klan, skinheads and neo-Nazis all started fighting, with accusations flying about of stealing members and mailing lists. By the time I arrived, my unity meeting was in shambles. As I looked out over the stormy proceedings, I realized: These groups wanted to "purify" the world and have it all be like them—but they hated one another. Did I really want to live in a world of people like that?

Were those the people I wanted to be my family? A family whose hate extended to all colors, backgrounds and ages? Even babies like Reverend Wade Watts's little daughter Tia? "How can you hate this child?" he had asked.

How far I had come from the days when I sang those words: "Jesus loves the little children, All the children of the world . . ."

Suddenly I was repulsed by the poison that swirled around me. I felt sick to my stomach. I turned in disgust and walked out the door. Eventually I told the other Klan officials I was giving up my position and leaving the group for good.

My life was a wreck. As the weeks passed, filled by a sense of shame and worthlessness, I fell into a deep depression—and the stultifying numbness of alcohol. Then came the terrible day I found myself in my shabby apartment raising a loaded gun to my head. *Daddy, I'm following in your footsteps. There's no other way to go . . .*

I was about to pull the trigger when I saw sunlight break through the partially closed blinds—and onto a Bible that lay gathering dust on my bookshelf, an old Bible like the one Reverend Wade Watts carried that day at the radio station. A Bible like the one I had seen my grandmother read so many times. *Maybe there is another way.* I put down the gun and picked up the Bible. It fell open to Luke 15—the parable of the prodigal son. I read the story three times, then fell on my knees and wept.

I quietly joined a church—whose congregation was multiracial—and kept a low profile, studying the Scripture, getting grounded in God's Word. Two years passed. And finally in 1991 I made a phone call I had to make.

"Reverend Watts?" I asked when he picked up.

He knew my voice right away. "Hello, Johnny Lee," he said warmly.

"Reverend Watts, I . . . I want you to know that I resigned from the KKK two years ago. I gave my heart to Jesus and I'm a member of an interracial church."

"Praise the Lord!" he shouted. "I've never stopped praying for you! Would you do me the honor of speaking at my church?"

How can he forgive me? How could he have cared about me all those years?

When I stepped to the podium at his church and looked out over the congregation of mostly black faces, I told my story simply, not hiding from the past or sugarcoating the depth and bitterness of my involvement. Then I told them how God had changed all the hate in my heart to love.

There was silence when I finished. A teenage girl got to her feet and ran down the aisle toward me, arms open. I started to move in front of the altar, to pray with her. As I passed the Reverend, I realized he was weeping. "Don't you know who that is, Johnny Lee?" he asked quietly. "That's Tia. That's my baby."

Yes, what I needed was a real family. And there had been one waiting to open its arms to me all along.

We have seen and testify that the Father has sent his Son to be the Savior of the world.

—1 JOHN 4:14 (NIV)

THE ROCK

by Barbara Fairchild

Most entertainers spend thousands of hours on the road. It's part of the job. The likelihood of accidents is a possibility that we live with on a daily basis. For me, that possibility became a reality one day in the mountains of Colorado.

I've been a singer nearly all my life. I entered my first talent show when I was five years old. Music was the rock that saw me through hard times and good times.

I wish I could say church was as important to me, but it wasn't. I was raised in St. Louis, in a strictly religious home, with emphasis on the strict. It seemed to me that nobody ever talked about *loving* God, just about following the rules.

As I got older and my rebellion became more noticeable, the list of things I couldn't do got longer. One night Mom insisted I make a choice: I could live my life right or plan on going to hell. At the time, my own desires seemed more real to me than hell did. I moved out and quit going to church.

To all appearances, things went well. I was able to make a living by singing. Often, while driving to club dates, I found myself thinking. I was on the road a lot. What if I had an accident? I was afraid of dying and I didn't want to go to hell, so I vowed to be extra careful on the roads.

Soon the focus of my career moved to Nashville. Frequently when I was there I stayed with a girlfriend of mine named Peggy, also a singer. She was one of those people who always smiled. Unless you knew her, you couldn't tell how terrible her life was. But this time she was so happy that I finally said, "What on earth has happened to you? I've never seen you so happy." She said, "I got saved."

Now in my old church we never talked about being saved, so I said, "Really, where? From what?" So she started talking about God and how He'd changed her life. She was going to church that night and she asked me to go along. I didn't have anything else to do, so I went. Before that week was out, Jesus invaded my life. I fell in love with Him and gave my life to Him.

My life changed. I stopped performing and became totally immersed in church activities to the exclusion of everything else.

Finally one day my husband said, "I'm just going to tell you one thing. Then I'm not going to bring it up anymore. If you think that God saved you so you could sit here on your behind and say 'Glory, hallelujah, I'm going to heaven when I die,' then you'd better think again. If every time a person becomes a Christian, he or she refuses to go where the people don't know about God, who's going to tell them?

"You know, Barbara, when I first met you, you were the sweetest person I'd ever known. But since you got religion you're the most selfish wretch I've ever seen. Why don't you start thinking about the people who need to hear what you sing?"

Well! That got me thinking, I'll tell you. The upshot was that I went back to singing.

But that meant I had to start traveling again. Shortly thereafter, I recorded "The Teddy Bear Song"—and watched, amazed, as it became a number one hit. Suddenly my concerts were in great demand, and our schedule necessitated that my band and I hit the road in a bus.

The bus was convenient, and even pleasant. We each had a bunk, and there was a television and a tape player to pass the time. I even brought along a mini-sewing machine. Things went well—until one fateful day.

It was late when we boarded the bus after the concert the night before. We'd been doing a series of concerts throughout Colorado. To reach our next destination in time to perform, we'd have to drive straight through without stopping. To do so, our professional driver had trained John, one of our band members, to drive the bus so the two of them could spell each other.

That night, I was bone tired and ready to sack out. As we started our ascent into the mountains, I managed to kick off my shoes before snuggling into the cocoon-warmth of my bunk in the back of the bus. Within moments I was asleep.

After several hours, the driver pulled over and woke John to spell him. The two of them went over the map and the route. Then we started off again.

Sometime later, John realized he must have missed the marked route. Rather than wake the driver, he looked at the map and found another road that looked possible. He didn't know that in the mountains roads can quickly become too narrow or too steep for a bus to negotiate. That's what happened. As the climb became steeper and steeper, the bus slowed to a crawl. Finally it couldn't go any farther. We came to a stop.

I awoke to the sudden stillness of the engine being shut off. It was overheated, and the driver decided to let it cool while finding the best way out of this predicament. Most of the band members woke up and got off the bus to study the problem. There was nothing I could do to help, so I drifted back to sleep.

In a few minutes I felt the bus start to move backward. I looked out of my bunk, and there was no driver at the wheel. Keith, my piano player, stuck his head out of his bunk too. "What's happening?" I asked.

"I'll go see," he said, and he jumped up. The driver forgot that the bus's air brakes were run by the engine. Once the air escaped, there was nothing holding us. The bus rolled backward, picking up more and more speed. We careered off the road. There were no trees on that slope, nothing to break our fall.

I was thrown from my bunk, tossed around like a rag doll. Keith came falling back my way. The pain was excruciating as I was slammed against the walls and bunks.

But then something incredible happened. In place of terror, I felt washed with a perfect peace. *This is the day I'll see the Lord,* I thought. From that moment I felt no pain.

The bus stopped. It was hanging onto a giant boulder by the front axle, tottering precariously. Keith and I stared at each other dumbly for a millisecond. Then we slowly and carefully started helping each other up the steep pitch of the bus aisle. When John reached the bus and climbed in to help us, his face told us we were still in danger.

When the three of us finally stood safe on solid ground, I saw how we'd been stopped in the middle of nothingness. I patted that boulder, and exclaimed, "Jesus is my rock!"

To this day, people think it incredible that my life was saved when the bus rolled off the mountain. But the real miracle wasn't that my life was saved; it's that God did not give up on the girl who gave up on Him years before. That day He even took away my fear of death. Today, though music is still an important part of me, I know that nothing can ever take the place of Jesus, the true Rock of my life.

A VISION OF GLORY

by Evelyn Bence

On Ascension Day I joined several friends for an informal spiritual retreat at Rehoboth Beach in Delaware. I was reading quietly when I was interrupted by a fellow retreatant. "Would you like to go for a walk?" she asked.

Not exactly what I had in mind. But sensing I needed to be less bookish, I smiled and said sure—let's. Was I surprised at the next hour's conversation.

She wanted to tell me what had happened to her there, at the beach, the previous spring. By the power of—in the name of—Jesus, she'd been released from years of nightmares and suicidal obsessions. A darkness had lifted; she'd been healed. Her story explained the lightness, even brightness, I'd noticed recently in her face and demeanor.

I thought that was the end of the story. There was more. Though she'd always been a spiritual person, she'd long ago discarded any notion that Jesus offered anything above and beyond other celebrated religious leaders. Any such claims could be chalked up to ignorance—or arrogance.

But the night after her healing, sitting beside her spiritual mentor on the Rehoboth boardwalk, she'd looked out over the Atlantic and caught a glimpse of eternity. In a vision, she'd seen the horizon open up. "I saw Jesus— standing on the right—reigning in glory. And in waves—like a circular arm combine—I saw everyone who had ever been born and ever would be born.

I saw Confucius, Buddha. Everyone. Millions. All centuries flashed by. And every person acknowledged that Jesus was Lord. Jesus stood apart, outside of the limits of time, eternal. Suddenly it was so obvious: What He had done— His incarnation, death and Resurrection—was once and for all. He wasn't one among many holy seers. He was—is—the Son of God, and He will come again when everyone has had the chance to hear His name."

I listened, amazed at what she'd seen where the ocean—the earth— met the sky. When her story wound to a close, I asked her if she knew an Ascension Day hymn by Caroline Noel, based on Philippians 2:10–11, "At the name of Jesus every knee shall bow. . . ."

She didn't. Later we found a hymnal and sang the long narrative: Jesus conquered death and then he

> Bore [his lordship] up triumphant
> > With its human light,
> Through all ranks of creatures,
> > To the central height,
> To the throne of Godhead,
> > To the Father's breast. . . .

We sang down to the last verse. She looked up at me, amazed, her eyes filled with tears: "That's what I saw! This is it."

> He is God the Savior,
> > He is Christ the Lord,
> Ever to be worshiped,
> > Trusted, and adored.

· PART 3 ·

Glimpses of Jesus
as Abiding Presence

THE NIGHT OF JESUS' RESURRECTION, as two of his disciples walked home to Emmaus, a "stranger" joined their company. He helped them understand the Scriptures; they wanted to hear more. At their front door, they invited him in, "Abide with us," they urged (Luke 24:29 KJV). Only later did they recognize the man as Jesus.

Abiding with us and in us. It's Jesus' deep desire: "Behold, I stand at the door and knock," he said, "if any one hears my voice and opens the door, I will come in to him and eat with him, and he with me" (Revelation 3:20 RSV).

We can get so caught up in our religious service and in our private agenda that we forget about the Christ who wants to—and does—abide in and with us. That's where the stories in this section begin. But by the end of this section, we glimpse the importance of sharing Jesus with others in their hours of need. There's something expansive about Christ's presence; as "Becky's Gift" poignantly illustrates, one can "give it away" without ever losing it.

WHO'S THERE?

by Sue Monk Kidd

When I worked as a nurse on the pediatric ward, before I listened to the little ones' chests, I would plug the stethoscope into their ears and let them listen to their own hearts beating. Their eyes would always light up with awe.

But I never got a response to equal four-year-old David's. I gently tucked the stethoscope inside his ears and placed the disk over his heart. "Listen," I said. "What do you suppose that is?"

He drew his eyebrows together in a puzzled line and looked up as if lost in the mystery of the strange tap-tap-tapping deep in his chest. Then his face broke out in a wondrous grin. "Is that Jesus knocking?" he said.

I smiled. Somewhere, maybe in Sunday school, David had obviously been told that lovely old illustration about Jesus standing at the door of our hearts, knocking.

Dear little David. You were exactly right. Inside your heart, and every heart, there is the faint, persistent sound of Jesus knocking. For Jesus comes to each of us every new day, wanting to share its moments with us. And maybe it is only those with the faith and wonder of a David who hear that knocking beneath the clamor of a busy world, and open the door.

MAY I COME IN?

by Adrian Plass

J esus' desire and willingness to move right into the homes and hearts of the sad, the bad and the greedy was and is a jewel in the crown of His ministry. The Pharisees were quite unable to accept it, and I imagine one or two of the sinners had a bit of a problem taking it in. They still do. I still do sometimes.

I remember, for instance, a particular fortnight around the end of August and beginning of September in the first year of this century.

The year had begun with the sad death of our dear dog Rosie who had grown up with our children, but being in the midst of hectic preparations for the blessing of my oldest son's marriage, we barely had a moment to mourn her passing. Matthew had married his charming Azeri bride Alina briefly (and technically) in Turkey earlier that year. Now they were anxious to do the marriage properly, and they wanted "the works." They wanted to be married by a proper vicar in a proper country church, wearing proper wedding clothes with proper guests and a proper wedding reception afterwards. And of course, ideally, it would happen on a proper sunny English day in early September.

Their wishes were granted. That year the second of September was one of those perfect days when nothing goes wrong and the laughter and tears and other weather all happen in just the right places. It couldn't have been more—proper.

A thrilling facet of this sparkling jewel of an occasion was the presence of Alina's parents, Irina and Oleg, who flew all the way from Baku, the capital of Azerbaijan, on the evening before the wedding to be with their daughter on her special day. Azerbaijan is a bureaucratic nightmare. Arranging visas and tickets had been a long, exhausting business for all of us. But now, excitingly, if improbably, these two non-English-speaking inhabitants of an oil-producing ex-Soviet republic were comfortably ensconced in a farmhouse bed-and-breakfast just down the road. Unbelievable!

It was in the week after the wedding that my neurosis began to set in. Our house had been occupied and eaten in every day by at least ten people, sometimes twelve. This was fine except that I am famous—or rather, infamous—for my dislike of clutter and untidiness. Members of my family alternate between derision and annoyance in their response to this aspect of my personality, but there's nothing I can do about it, I'm afraid. I am capable of a sort of cataclysmic untidiness of my own on rare occasions, but the point is that I select those occasions, if you see what I mean.

During that second week I began to understand how servants working in large houses in the Victorian and Edwardian eras must have felt during every day of their lives. Vacuuming and washing up and laying tables and putting things away and preparing meals and taking rubbish to the dump and shopping and sorting everything out was exhausting. Not, I hasten to add, in case my wife reads this, that I labored alone. We all worked hard. No, it was just that this completion neurosis of mine drove me past the point of reasonable endeavor, producing a state of wild-eyed frustration in me whenever some innocent soul committed the unforgivable sin of moving a coffee cup on a polished surface without using a coaster. Sad, isn't it?

For the first few days of this feverish activity, though I say it myself, I handled things pretty well. I quite enjoyed an inner, heroic posturing in the role of one working selflessly for the sake of others. I was the host who not only welcomed and entertained, but also labored ceaselessly behind the scenes with no thought of reward or gratitude. How impressed they must be, I reflected, by the way the house is magically sorted out in their absence each day, calm and ordered in readiness for their return. A good witness too, I thought smugly (may God forgive me!), for Christians to offer those from a distant, pagan land.

At around lunchtime on the thirteenth day I simply ran out of steam and goodwill. Why the dickens was I bothering to clean up after people who just came in and messed it all up again? What was the point? When were they going to acknowledge the hard work I'd been doing? They probably hadn't even noticed. Huh! Fancy coming all this way from a foreign country and letting me slave away like a—like a slave. I felt tired and irritable and fed up . . .

That morning I sat at my desk, head in hands, surveying the wreckage of my good intentions and the disintegration of my so-called Christian witness. The dwelling place of my faith was in a state of complete disarray, quite unsuitable for visitors. It was at that moment that the gentle voice of Jesus said, very quietly, "May I come in?"

"Well," I replied, almost tearfully, "it's a bit of a mess, actually."

"Oh, I've never minded that," he said, "I'll give you a hand clearing up."

"Thank you," I said, and I meant it.

He calls on the strangest people at the strangest times, doesn't He? Ready?

HEAD OF THE HOUSE?

by Kathryn Slattery

The old, homeless man stood on the corner of a sidewalk in Greenwich Village in New York City. Among the used magazines, tattered clothing and odds and ends he spread out to sell, a small plaque caught my eye: "Jesus Is the Head of My House."

The message was spelled out in silver letters that someone had glued on a five-by-seven-inch scrap of cardboard and then decorated with cutouts of strawberry-patterned wallpaper. The glass was dirty, the gray paint on the wooden frame was flaking. Maybe the old man had made the plaque himself.

"Is two dollars all right?" I asked, fishing in my purse.

He nodded. I gave him the money and tucked the plaque in a diaper bag slung over the back of the stroller where my son slept. Then I hurried home.

Even after I cleaned the glass and wiped the frame with a damp cloth, the plaque was dingy. So I hung it on a hook in our bedroom closet, where it played peekaboo through the hangers.

As the years passed and our children grew, the old plaque moved with us from our first apartment on Horatio Street, crosstown to our co-op on East Eleventh Street, where I hung it on a nail above the laundry tub.

Then my husband Tom and I decided to move to the suburbs, where raising our children would be easier and less expensive. But caught in the

Manhattan real-estate crash, we were unable to sell our co-op—even at a huge loss. So we rented a run-down house in Connecticut, and the plaque went on a cobwebby windowsill in the cellar. One winter's day I found it face up on the linoleum floor, its glass broken into shards.

"Jesus Is the Head of My House." Illuminated by the harsh glare of a naked bulb, the words seemed to mock me. *What house?* I wondered.

I hated the place we were renting. Cold in the winter, buggy in summer, it bore the scars of tenant neglect. The harvest-gold paint on the outside was peeling, and the avocado-green shutters were rotting.

Tom's family had mailed us a handsome personalized doormat for a housewarming present, but I couldn't bring myself to put it out. This was not our home. I was ashamed to welcome any guests. More times than I cared to admit, I'd picked up the phone to ask someone over for coffee or supper and changed my mind at the last minute.

Sometimes I felt guilty for being unhappy. After all, we had much to be thankful for. We had found a good church. Our children, Katy and Brinck, were thriving at their new elementary school and making new friends. They relished the freedom of a backyard and loved riding their bikes up and down the block. Tom didn't even mind the hour-plus commute on the train. We enjoyed the slower pace of life, the sound of wind in the trees, the red flash of a cardinal or the sight of deer nibbling at the rhododendron bushes.

Now I looked at the broken plaque lying on the basement floor. Gingerly I picked up a splinter of glass and tossed it into a plastic trash pail. I reached for another shard and tossed it, then another. Finally the glass was gone, but the framed message was still there: "Jesus Is the Head of My House."

And I got the message at last. It was as though someone spoke the words with a forcefulness that jolted me out of my gloom. *Of course!* My house was not this leaky, creaky structure built on top of dreary concrete blocks. My house was not our unsold co-op in the city, nor would it be the suburban Colonial we dreamed of buying someday.

My house is my heart. Every day I had the privilege of inviting Jesus to be the head—filling me with His hope, encouragement, guidance and love. My fingers traced the silver letters. Jesus hadn't been the Head of my house for a long time.

Lord, I prayed, *I'm so sorry I've shut you out. Please come into my heart and be the Head of my house.*

I returned the plaque to its spot on the windowsill. Turning to go, I noticed a pile of boxes stacked under the basement stairwell. It took some rummaging, but I found what I was looking for. Running upstairs, I opened the front door and rolled out the doormat. "The Slatterys," it said.

Would we ever sell our co-op? Would we ever own a home again? Somehow those questions didn't seem to matter much anymore. I headed to the kitchen to phone a friend from church and invite her over for coffee. I was ready to be welcoming. Thanks to a homeless man, I knew where my home was—and to whom it belonged.

"I WANTED TO BE OPEN"

by Patricia Chapman

One warm spring day we planted a small olive tree in the patio of our Southern California home. It was positioned so we could keep track of its growth through the tall windows that framed the fireplace on the east end of the living room.

The early morning sun streamed in through those windows, but as time passed and the olive tree grew, its branches began to filter out the penetrating rays. At first the shade was sparse, but with each passing year we were sheltered more and more from the sun.

One day I was having my devotions in the living room. It was quiet in the house—the girls were on their way to school and my husband was at the office. Suddenly I felt impressed with the presence of the Lord inside the room. I got up off my knees and walked, still in a prayerful mood, to the end of the living room, and looked at the olive tree. I had been telling the Lord that I was open to the fullness of His Spirit and to fill me in any way He chose. I wanted to be open to whatever God had for me.

Without warning, a gust of wind shook the little tree violently for a few moments, and then it was still and quiet again. As I reflected on what happened, it seemed to me that God was present in this incident. I felt that He was speaking to me in a very real and special way as I remembered that the oil of the olive berry was a symbol of the Holy Spirit, as is the wind. God had, I believed, answered my prayer with the assurance that He was indeed with me now in His Fullness.

This was an amazing experience for me. Nothing like that had ever happened before to me, nor has it since. I know now that I must have felt like the people in the crowd when Jesus healed the paralyzed man who had been let down through the roof while Jesus was teaching. Mark described their reaction this way: ". . . they were all amazed, and glorified God, saying, We never saw it on this fashion" (Mark 2:12 KJV).

Sometimes Jesus' spirit speaks in a dramatic way to us as He spoke to me through the olive tree and the whirlwind. Sometimes He touches the suffering and heals. At other times He doesn't seem to speak at all. Yet His presence is with us. . . . We can be certain that as we seek Him out, He will minister to each of us in His way and in His time.

I pray that Christ will be
more and more at home in your hearts,
living within you as you trust in him. . . .
—EPHESIANS 3:17 (TLB)

JESUS AND JOY: A PICTURE IN THE WALLET OF MY HEART

by Mike Mason

In October 1999 I began a ninety-day experiment in joy. I made up my mind that for the next ninety days I would be joyful in the Lord. Because this was an experiment, there was room for failure. If there were times when I wasn't joyful, I wouldn't despair or beat myself up. Rather I would gently, persistently return as best I could to my focus on joy.

Happiness has not been my strong suit, which is why I needed to experiment with joy.

In April 1994, five years before I began my experiment, I had a vision of Jesus. I was praying with a friend in my living room when suddenly Jesus stood before me. Though I call this a "vision," what happened was so utterly, fantastically real that it didn't seem like a vision at all. Purely and simply, I met Jesus of Nazareth face to face. There was no doubt in my mind that it really was He; I would have known Him anywhere.

I wasn't feeling particularly holy that day, indeed the opposite. A few hours later I'd be getting on a plane to join my parents for their fiftieth wedding anniversary, and I was preoccupied with plans for this event. I hadn't yet packed, I had a hundred details to attend to, and my mind was further distracted by my daughter's loud music in the next room. Hardly the setting for a quiet prayer time. When my friend suggested we pray, I agreed merely to humor him.

In this unlikely setting Jesus appeared to me. I've never had another vision, before or since, but this one so affected me that I carry it with me always like a photo in the wallet of my heart. I see Him again now as I write, especially His face. If I were an artist I would paint Him. As it is, I'll say only that Jesus did not resemble any of the popular images I've seen. Rather, He was just as Isaiah described him: "He had no beauty or majesty to attract us to him, nothing in his appearance that we should desire him" (Isaiah 53:2 NIV). Yes, the Jesus I saw is a decidedly unhandsome man. With any ordinary human, one might almost apply the word *ugly*—except Jesus is not ugly. He's beautiful. He's so radiant and loving that all normal standards of physical beauty are disqualified.

What mainly struck me was His joy. He was positively beaming with happiness, like ten thousand suns, and I felt that all this joy was directed at me. He was so glad to see me! Moreover He was inviting me to share His happiness.

I felt some response was called for—but what? I wanted to say something to my Lord, yet talking to the real, visible Jesus is quite different from saying prayers in an empty room. "Oh, Lord," I stammered, "it's so good to be with You. . . ." Whatever I said came out sounding lame. Stupid, forced, artificial. Here I was with the chance of a lifetime and I was blowing it royally. Who did I think I was, seeing and talking to Jesus Christ?

At that point my vision faded. For a while I kept still, trying to bring Him back. But no, the experience was over. When eventually I opened my eyes I was back in the living room with my friend. The loud music was still playing and everything was the same as before. Yet everything was different because now I was filled with joy. I was ecstatic!

Somehow I got my bag packed and made it to the airport, and throughout the four-hour plane ride I leaned back in the chair and dreamed of Jesus, picturing His face again and again, studying Him from every angle. And after that I enjoyed the most wonderful visit I've ever had with my parents, celebrating their fifty years of marriage. I didn't tell anyone my experience; I didn't have to. I'd been filled with the joy of the Lord, and because of this all my contacts with people over the next few days took on a wholly different quality.

Nevertheless, while the joy of the vision stayed with me for several days, I couldn't live there. Normal life resumed, and in time I found myself reflecting less on Jesus' happiness than on my own awkwardness. I felt bad because, face to face with the Lord, I hadn't known how to talk to Him, let alone how to share His joy. And so I was left with a sense of incompletion, which gradually modulated into an invitation.

He was inviting me to share His happiness. At the time my faith was too halting, my self-doubt too strong even to imagine entering into a life of sustained joy. Yet an invitation from Jesus is a powerful summons, and now, by His grace, I have answered His call.

The following is Mike's description of Day 67 of his experiment in joy.

Day 67 of my experiment fell on January 1, 2000, widely celebrated as the dawn of the new millennium. That New Year's Eve we sat with friends around a campfire beside a frozen lake in the interior of British Columbia. At midnight we watched in wonder as bursts of fireworks, dramatically illuminating the falling snow, flowered in the vast, dark whiteness.

On the stroke of twelve we toasted the new millennium with a bottle of sparkling apple juice, and I had what I can only describe as a mystical experience. As I raised the glass to my lips and drank, I felt I had never before tasted anything so delicious. The juice was like an ambrosial nectar, exquisitely refreshing, even intoxicating (though it contained no alcohol). It was as if that bottle held the very essence of my surroundings on that unique night—the dark frozen wilderness, the bright falling snow, the bursting fireworks, the cool bite of winter in the air, the gentle warmth of friends around a campfire. Mix all these together in a drink, along with a hint of something exotic and unnameable, and the taste came as near as I can imagine to the taste of joy itself—truly a champagne for the soul.

Joy filled me that night, and again in the morning upon awakening to a world of sparkling whiteness. The whole lake was covered in a blanket of clean new snow, not a mark on it. This beautiful symbol of a brand-new millennium was matched by a feeling of clean freshness and limitless possibility in my own spirit. Perhaps this is the pinnacle of earthly joy—this sensation of pure oneness with one's surroundings, of complete harmony between inner and outer worlds.

A similar sense of mystical oneness with the physical world came over me many times during my experiment in joy. Sometimes joy came through contemplating spiritual truths or through overcoming problems of an abstract nature. Just as often, however, I found the vehicle of joy was something thoroughly physical—a painting, a piece of music, a flower, a hug or a touch, a drink of sparkling apple juice. At times I might seem to derive nothing from an hour of prayer, only to go outside and discover the joy of the Lord in the wind on my face. Often I sat down to meals that seemed the best I'd ever eaten. Yes, there were good friends around the table and many spiritual reasons to be happy, yet it wouldn't have been the same without the physical presence of roast beef and gravy . . . and chocolate cupcakes. Nehemiah knew this when he told his people, "Go and enjoy choice food and sweet drinks . . . for the joy of the Lord is your strength" (Nehemiah 8:10 NIV).

To the Christian, the physical and the spiritual are not separate but complementary. To be spiritually alive and happy is to find the physical senses awakening as never before. Nothing is more physical than the incarnation, death, Resurrection and ascension of Jesus. Because our awesome Creator God made this world with His own hands and further hallowed it by living here Himself, joy is free to take full delight in earthly existence, fleeting though it may be—just as Jesus did when He turned water into wine at a wedding feast. If ever any drink was more delicious than the one I tasted that New Year's Eve, surely it was the champagne of Cana with which Jesus inaugurated the kingdom of heaven.

Is it really possible to be happy all the time? Three years after my experiment, I still cannot quite join Brother Lawrence in saying, "I am always very happy." What I can say is that every day is full of moments of happiness, as full as the sky is of stars. Yes, an immense expanse of cold black space yawns out there, but that's not what draws my eye anymore. My gaze, and with it my understanding, has shifted. To believe in God is to believe in good and to see its preponderance everywhere. All I see now are the bright, jewel-like moments of joy that keep coming to me and that, taken together, do not seem a jumble of random sparks, but comprise a great and dazzling picture—a vision so beautiful as to utterly overwhelm the darkness.

I THANK GOD FOR THE GIFT

by Zona B. Davis

I first met Ruth one Sunday evening when I volunteered to take her to her shelter-care home after church services. The home was adjacent to a busy highway and I asked her, "Does the noise of the traffic bother you?"

"Oh no," she said quickly. "I like living by the highway and watching the people pass by. I like to wonder where they came from and I try to imagine where they're going. I thank God that He gave me plenty of imagination!"

Later Ruth was moved to another room where a wing of the building cut off her view of everything but an enormous, spreading tree. "Maybe you should ask for a different room," I suggested.

"Oh no," she said, "I like this one. That big old tree has many stories to tell me . . . about storms that it has weathered, and lightning and cold snows and singing birds and frisky squirrels. I do thank God for the gift of imagination!"

Then Ruth was transferred to another shelter-care home in town. "You've lost your big tree," I sympathized.

"Oh, this is fine," she told me. "I can watch the children playing outdoors . . . it brings back such wonderful memories. Also, there's a senior-citizens center only two blocks away and I often go over there to visit friends and enjoy a cup of tea."

"Well, let's hope you won't have to move again," I told her with a sigh.

"Oh, that's all right—Jesus always moves with me," she smiled, her blue eyes shining. "He brings me my *imagination*!"

---

*Floods of joy o'er my soul
like the sea billows roll,
Since Jesus came into my heart.*

—RUFUS MCDANIEL

BECKY'S GIFT

by Christina Mazmanian

F rom now on," the receptionist told my parents, "when you bring Rebekah to the hospital, please use the rear entrance. Take the elevator right up to the third floor and try not to let anyone see her."

The third floor was where the "undesirable" children were sent, children with obvious birth defects. "It upsets the other patients to see your daughter," the woman said. And then she herself looked away.

This all took place in the 1960s, in a small town in central New Jersey, when I was twelve. There were already four children in our family, girls ranging in age from eight to sixteen, when our mother told us another baby was coming. We never tired of pressing our hands against our mother's belly when the baby kicked. When we should have been asleep, we were still awake in bed, talking about how we would take turns feeding and holding our baby.

The baby finally came—and it was twins! The infants were named Rebekah and Rachel, and they could not have been more loved.

Rachel had beautiful eyes, pudgy cheeks, and a little round head covered with peach fuzz that I loved to kiss.

Rebekah's body was tiny, but her head was so large that I thought her neck would break from the weight of it. She had bulging veins and sunken eyes that held a haunting look of suffering.

Rebekah was hydrocephalic. She had a condition more commonly known as "water on the brain." Too much fluid had collected in her skull, causing extreme pain and epileptic seizures.

At first, it was hard to look at Rebekah. But then she would smile and it was as though a candle had been lit in a dark room. That smile would light up her entire face and then spread to light up the heart of the person lucky enough to see it.

One day my music teacher asked me to stay after class. I was hoping to get the lead singing role in the upcoming school play, and I was sure this was what she wanted to talk about. But instead she sighed and told me she was sorry about my baby sister. "What a terrible thing someone in your family must have done," she said. "If you were the good girl I thought you were, you would ask God to heal your sister. God always answers the prayers of a righteous girl."

My knees felt as if they were going to buckle. Could it be my fault my sister was the way she was? I went home and cried for hours in my room. I had asked God to heal my sister many times. Now, every time Rebekah cried out in pain or had a seizure, my teacher's words echoed in my ears.

For such a tender spirit as mine, this was more than I could bear. Perhaps I could have found comfort in prayer. But feeling that God was angry with me filled me with such shame that I couldn't pray. God seemed very, very far from me.

One cold night baby Rebekah once again had to be taken to the hospital. My mom was in the ambulance with her, and my dad was following in the car. I stood on our front porch watching the ambulance lights fade away.

I didn't know how I could face the future, thinking that I was the cause of all this suffering my family was forced to endure. Falling to my knees, I cried out, "Where are You, God? How could You leave me all alone?"

Everything around me was completely still. I wiped my eyes and I looked up.

It was then I saw the star. At first just a twinkle high in the sky, it began to shine with an unreal brightness. I was mesmerized by its brilliance. Slowly it took the distinct shape of a cross. It was, without any doubt, a brightly shining cross. I felt surrounded by love. Then I heard, as clearly as if they were spoken out loud, these words: *I could never leave you, nor will I ever leave you. Fear not. For I am with you always.*

I am not sure how long I stayed on the porch that night. It must have been a long time, for I was very cold when I finally went inside. Yet I felt a warmth in my heart that I had never felt before.

I never told anyone about my extraordinary "cross." I wanted to hug the feeling of peace and love within myself; it was too precious to share.

By the time she was four, Rebekah had had countless brain surgeries. In those days hospitals had very strict visiting hours, and parents and families were not allowed to stay overnight. When we left her, big tears would roll down Rebekah's cheeks and her body would shake with sobs. I remember crying for most of the ride home.

In time, though, Rebekah gained courage from a picture of Jesus that was always taped to the foot of her bed. "My Jesus is with me," she would say. "My Jesus loves me, Mommy. He hugs me at night. My Jesus is here." And she would pat her little chest, just over her heart.

In Rebekah's room one day was a young girl about to undergo brain surgery. She was eight years old and very frightened. She began to cry and became hysterical. Even her parents could not comfort her.

Four-year-old Rebekah was recovering from yet another surgery. I remember her sitting quietly with a serious look on her face. Then suddenly she smiled.

"I know what to do," she told my mother in a whisper. She climbed down from Mom's lap and slowly walked over to the girl.

"Don't cry," she said softly, rubbing the girl's cheek. "I was afraid too. But I'm not afraid anymore."

By now the girl was quietly crying as Rebekah continued to stroke her cheek. "Why aren't you afraid now?" the older child asked between sobs.

"Because I have my Jesus," Rebekah said. "No one has to be afraid if they have my Jesus." She raised both of her hands to her heart and held them like a cup, as if scooping water from a fountain to drink.

"Here," she said, "open your hands for me."

The other girl had stopped sobbing and was totally involved in their conversation. Solemnly she reached out as Rebekah transferred her most treasured possession into the cupped hands of her friend.

"Take my Jesus," she said. "If my Jesus is with you, you won't be afraid. But I need Him too, so bring Him back when your operation is over."

The girl smiled. She leaned to kiss Rebekah's swollen face. Then she clasped her hands to her own chest and held them there as she was wheeled out.

The little girl did not return from the operation. Her mother and father were the ones who carried Rebekah's Jesus back to her, returning His presence as gently and reverently as Becky had delivered it hours before. How much easier it was, they said, knowing their daughter had left them with smiles and peace instead of tears and fear.

Rebekah's entire life on this earth was spent in giving her Jesus to everyone she met. Not one day was lived without pain; she went through so many operations that even my parents lost count. And yet nurses, doctors, friends and family all saw a glimpse of God's wondrous love through Rebekah.

She died at the age of twenty-one, and I am filled with thanksgiving that I was her sister.

And I am filled with thanksgiving for a God who cradled my "undesirable" sister in the palm of His hand. A God who gave my parents a strength that held our family together through those fearful years. A God who cared enough to comfort a troubled twleve-year-old by putting into the night sky a glittering star as a symbol of His love. And who brought peace to suffering children by the pure unfailing flow of His abiding Spirit.

Help of the helpless,
O abide with me.

—HENRY LYTE

AUNT ALTA'S EASTER LESSON

by Marilyn Morgan King

When I was a teenager, I went through a period of questioning my faith. Luckily, I had an aunt who wasn't afraid of questions. Once, just before Easter, I asked Aunt Alta about Christ's Resurrection. "How do we *know* Jesus really came back from the dead? The Bible says He did, but how can we be sure those people didn't just say they saw Him?" Aunt Alta took me outside to a clump of gray, dead-looking bushes by the fruit cellar door, cut off a couple of branches, and brought them in the house. In three days, those dead-looking twigs blossomed into a profusion of bright yellow, gloriously living flowers. Then Aunt Alta explained to me that, just as the forsythia bloomed when we brought it in the house, I needed to bring Christ into the center of my life. She said that if I'd do that I could know, *firsthand*, that the Resurrection was true, because His living presence would blossom within me.

Whenever I find myself thinking of Jesus only as Someone who lived two thousand years ago, I remember Aunt Alta's forsythia and try to let Him back into the center of my life, where His living presence blossoms anew, dispelling my doubts. When the branches of your faith seem gray and lifeless, try bringing Christ back into the "living room" of your soul and let Him spring to life there.

· PART 4 ·

Glimpses of Jesus as Wounded Healer

JESUS, THE GREAT PHYSICIAN. This isn't a biblical phrase, yet it harkens to the Gospel accounts of Jesus' ministry: healing the sick—bodies and also souls. In Luke 5:31–32 (NIV) Jesus talked about this role: "It is not the healthy who need a doctor, but the sick. I have not come to call the righteous, but sinners to repentance."

The following stories give glimpses of Jesus as physical and spiritual Healer. Lynda Jamison's recovery from depression, which had contributed to obesity, started when she saw and suddenly understood the meaning behind a crucifix: Jesus saying, *I died for you. Give me your pain.* The prophet Isaiah described a suffering servant who would take up our infirmities, "by his wounds we are healed" (Isaiah 53:5 NIV). In an insightful piece aptly titled "Closer to Him," Elizabeth Sherrill discusses why God allows suffering. We then turn to some dramatic examples of healing, from which we can learn new lessons of faith, as we glimpse God's presence and power.

TOO POWERFUL TO IGNORE

by Lynda Jamison

Backstage, I smoothed the gray sequined pantsuit over my still-large frame, panic filling me. *I haven't lost enough weight. What if I talk too much between songs? I won't remember the words . . .*

Beyond the stage door were friends, family and many faces that had become familiar over the last few years as I hopscotched across East Coast nightspots. They had come to the biggest booking of my new career at one of cabaret's most hallowed halls—the Oak Room in New York City's Algonquin Hotel. This was a dream I had once given up for marriage. Now my husband was out there with our two grown sons. I leaned against the door, my heart racing, and marveled at the twists and turns of the long path that had led me here . . .

A girl of five, I am sitting next to Mother on a mahogany bench at her grand piano. The afternoon sun slants through the tall windows, making her long blond hair glisten and casting a yellow glow on the reams of sheet music stacked on the piano. She is so pretty, my mother, and her sure hands and flawless lyric soprano turn the room into a magical place. We are singing together, and as her fingers dance across the keys, a surge of excitement courses through me and makes my body tingle.

I grew up surrounded by music: Mom's singing, and the piano she or my sister or I played. Then there were the records—Rosemary Clooney,

Shirley Jones, Julie Andrews, Margaret Whiting. When music wasn't playing in our house it played in my head. It was my world.

I was seven years old and we were on a train when Mom told me Daddy had gone off to live with another woman and was never coming back. I was crushed. In tears I crawled underneath the covers in my Pullman berth. Even then there was music: the train clickety-clacking, "He's never coming back again; he's never coming back again."

After Daddy left I gave myself over to music completely. It took away the hurt and loneliness.

Three years later Mom got remarried to a wonderful man. He loved us, and the music in our house became joyous again.

One cold winter night he took us to New York's Radio City Music Hall with my aunt and my grandmother. We got dressed up, and I felt so grand in the huge theater with all the lights and a stage that seemed to stretch for miles. The giant Wurlitzer appeared from a side wall and began to fill the room with chords that resonated in my ribs. Suddenly dozens of Rockettes were onstage high-kicking. When I was ten years old in Radio City Music Hall, my dream was born. After the show I raced up to our hotel room and gazed into the mirror over the bureau. I saw myself as an adult—a singer with my name in lights on a Broadway marquee.

Every free moment I had I practiced, danced, sang, acted and studied for a career in music. Then one day, when I was twenty, I met him. Six feet four, blond, blue-eyed, a fabulous dancer, gentle yet strong, Bob Jamison had a smile that made me melt. Mom said, "Don't let this one get away." She needn't have worried. We fell in love fast, and Bob proposed twenty-eight days after our first date.

A week before he proposed, I had auditioned for Beatrice Krebs, the head of the voice department at Carnegie Tech University. The day after I said yes to Bob's all-important question, Miss Krebs called and said she wanted to send me to New York City for two auditions she was certain would result in work. I was giddy at the prospect. I couldn't understand the frown that wrinkled Mom's brow. "What about Bob?" she asked.

"What about him?" I shuddered, already dreading her answer.

"You can't have both. It won't work." She had been a radio and night-club singer and knew the demands of a career onstage.

As much as I loved Bob, the choice hurt. I skipped the auditions and gave up my career, but prayed the music would keep on playing in my life.

After a storybook wedding, Bob and I set up housekeeping in a nice neighborhood of tidy yards and shady maples in suburban Pittsburgh. I threw myself into wifedom, making our house comfortable and cooking gourmet meals. Rob and Tim came along, wonderful boys, and I adored being a mother.

Yet the place I had filled with music was empty. I tried to escape it by becoming active in our church, joining the Junior League and garden club. I helped at Little League and Cub Scouts, and organized church suppers, bazaars and fund-raisers. I ran, ran, ran from the void that dogged me. While returning from carpooling a bunch of kids to Scouts one afternoon, I was singing along to a Rosemary Clooney tape when suddenly I lost it. "Lord," I screamed, "why did you give me a beautiful voice and then not let me use it?" Immediately I felt ashamed, but that didn't stop the ache.

I began to try to fill the void with food. I grew disgusted with myself for compulsive overeating, then went on rigorous diets that I always broke, ending up heavier than ever. One morning I was putting breakfast dishes in the washer. Idly I picked up a half-eaten doughnut and finished it. Ten minutes later I had finished the whole box of doughnuts, as well as a half gallon of jamoca almond fudge ice cream. Even though my stomach felt as if it were about to burst, the emptiness inside gnawed at me, and self-loathing rushed through me. I was forty-four years old, weighed 319 pounds, and lived in tent dresses.

I cried all day. When Bob came home I told him, "I need help."

He put his arms around me and said, "I'm with you and so is God."

I left for thirty days for a treatment center in California. At this place there were no committees or fund-raisers. No refrigerator. No music. Just me and my feelings. One afternoon between therapy sessions, I followed a pebbled path and sat on a tree-shaded wood bench that faced a crucifix. I stared at the tortured form of Christ for a long time. I had never dwelled on Christ's pain, but the longer I looked, the more I felt it. Then it was almost as if He were speaking to me: *I died for that little girl hiding under the covers in the Pullman berth. I have the power to heal her, but you must give her to Me.*

Mentally I turned the knob on the door that closed off the empty place deep inside me. "Please take her," I whispered. "Take all of me." I felt the peace of God flowing through me.

It was a beginning. The image of Jesus' sacrifice was too powerful for me to ignore. He didn't think I was disgusting. Neither did Bob. By the time I got home I had the courage to face the empty pang within. I joined Overeaters Anonymous. Within a year I was sixty pounds lighter and still losing weight. "With God everything is possible" became my watchwords.

A year later Bob and I were in our den having after-dinner coffee. We talked with the easy familiarity of old friends who love each other very much. I studied his kind face with its strong jaw and its thick shock of white hair. It made me happy just to look at him. We were in a good place. I had so much to be thankful for.

The telephone rang. It was a friend of Bob's who ran the Fox Chapel Follies, a large amateur theatrical production held every three years as a charity benefit. "Lynda," he said, "I'm hoping you'll audition this year."

My stomach dropped. "I haven't performed in twenty-eight years. I don't think I—"

"Hey, I've heard you sing around a piano at a party. You're good," he persisted.

Could this be my second chance? I wondered. I turned to Bob. "He wants me to audition for the Fox Chapel Follies."

"Seems like God's perfect timing to me," he said with a grin that filled the room. "Do it."

I got the lead singing part, and afterward was booked at Cardillo's Club Cafe in Pittsburgh. Bob bought me a sound system and pretty soon he was driving me up and down the East Coast to singing engagements. Three years later I was offered my own show in the Oak Room of the Algonquin Hotel.

That's how I found myself nervously smoothing my gray sequined suit, trembling like a teenager on the brink of a thirty-year-old dream. Because I had finally dared to stop running and trust myself entirely to God's leading, I was about to live that dream. I stepped through the stage door to a burst of applause. Down in front, white hair gleaming, blue eyes misty, was the dearest face in the world. I blew him a kiss and sang from my heart my first song.

"Daughter, your faith has healed you.
Go in peace and be freed
from your suffering."
—MARK 5:34 (NIV)

CLOSER TO HIM

by Elizabeth Sherrill

By age twenty-two, I'd experienced various kinds of pain—everything from family bereavement to root canal surgery without anesthetics. But there was one kind of suffering I'd never imagined . . . the pain of feeling betrayed by God.

If I thought of God at all, it was only to dismiss His existence. Then, in Fleetwood, New York, where my husband John and I had settled into our first apartment, I came across this type of suffering for the first time. Though it's been more than fifty years since we lived next door to Henry and Martha, I can still hear Henry's anguished question, "What did Martha ever do that God should punish her so?"

Martha—only three years older than I at the time—was dying of cancer of the spine. Henry didn't need to describe her agony. The apartment walls were thin. His wife's pain, though so much worse than anything I'd experienced, was at least something I could relate to. Henry's was not. The idea of pain as punishment had never even occurred to me.

On the contrary, I'd learned from a college dormmate at Northwestern the important function pain served in daily life. Lucinda's mother had an illness that rendered her unable to feel pain. She couldn't tell when water scalded or when she stepped on something sharp. A human guardian was needed to do the work that pain does for the rest of us.

But pain served no protecting purpose in our next-door neighbor's situation. Martha suffered a brutal, unceasing torture. Henry's response was to rage at God.

Unbearable though my own painful episodes had seemed as I was going through them, I hadn't held God responsible. You can't be angry at someone you don't believe in. But Henry and Martha were deeply religious. "She never missed a Sunday at church!" was one of Henry's bitterest cries.

When, some years later, I took my own first tentative steps in faith, the memory of Henry's torment was the chief obstacle I wrestled with. If I were to believe in an all-good, all-powerful God, I too would confront the why of such suffering as Martha's. Pain would become not only a physical and emotional ordeal, but a spiritual one as well.

Searching for answers, John and I began attending various churches to find some of the ways believers deal with the dilemma of suffering.

In one place we were told that pain was only an illusion of the mind. When I had to take our two-year-old daughter Liz, who had an excruciating earache, out of the service, we were followed to the church parking lot by several members of the congregation. They told us reproachfully that the cause of her suffering was not an infection, but my belief that the ache was real.

We met others who saw pain as a wake-up call. Several years after we left the Fleetwood apartment, John underwent cancer surgery. He was visited in the hospital by the pastor of a church we'd attended a few months previously. The postoperative pain John was feeling was a foretaste—a mild foretaste, the man stressed—of the pains of hell awaiting those who've turned their backs on God.

Still others saw pain as a teaching device. "I think God was telling you not to climb so high," a technician told our eight-year-old son Scott as she X-rayed his broken arm.

Pain as punishment, pain as a creation of the mind, pain as warning, pain as schoolmaster—I could find some sense in all these interpretations. A stomachache will punish me for an eating binge. My mental attitude does affect how much something hurts. A chest pain may remind me of my mortality. And every experience teaches.

But none of these explanations completely satisfied me. Pain often has nothing to do with what I've eaten or anything else I do. Animals don't "believe" in pain, but they surely experience it. Pain may drive some to seek God who otherwise would not, but it also afflicts the devout. And often teaches us what we know only too well.

Yet pain played a role in my own commitment to Jesus. An experience of John's moved our search for God out of the realm of the theoretical.

During a second cancer surgery in 1959, John's lungs collapsed while he was on the operating table and a four-hour battle for his life was waged over his unconscious form. All that John knew, waking in the recovery room, was that a cat's cradle of tubes protruded from his chest and that he was in the most intense pain of his life. The pain was not only physical but emotional, as he assumed the cancer, which in fact had been contained, must have metastasized throughout his chest.

Into that pain-filled place came Jesus. He came as light, "light, impossibly bright," John told me later, "light that was a being." And in that radiant presence, John's first thought, to his own amazement, was to pray for others in the recovery room whose moans he'd been hearing. Immediately, the moans ceased.

John's own pain, though, did not. Hadn't he asked Jesus, I wanted to know, to take away the pain? But he had not. He had encountered something infinitely more compelling than pain, and in the joy and wonder of that meeting, pain had ceased to be his focus.

It was the beginning, for both of us, of a relationship with God. Stunned by John's experience, I began to read the Bible and discovered that the mystery of suffering has occupied far wiser minds than mine ever since Adam and Eve were driven from the garden.

In the Bible's sixty-six books, I came across many portrayals of God's role in pain. I found the God of wrath, whose lightning bolts may be averted with gifts. I met the righteous Judge, sending just punishment on a guilty people. But I also saw the compassionate God, in both the Old and New Testaments, who heals His people's pain rather than causes it.

One of the most famous examinations of the issue is in the Book of Job. Written centuries before the birth of Christ, the story asks, as our neighbor Henry did: Why do the righteous suffer? Pious, prayerful Job had been assaulted by overwhelming physical and emotional agony. His friends insisted that such pain must be punishment for some secret sin. Or a warning against pride.

Although Job never resolves the why of pain, he rejects these simplistic answers, maintaining his faith in a God of love. So do the scores of faithful people I've met in writing for Guideposts for over half a century—people with lives and bodies ravaged by war, accident, illness . . . but with spirits that radiate joy.

All attest that suffering has brought them closer to God. I too find as time goes by—I find right now in the arthritis that makes me shift as I write—that the why of pain becomes less important than something else. Someone else.

The figure of Jesus on the cross has become, for me, the answer to the question Henry first made me consider: How can I believe in a loving God in a hurting world? I like to think that Henry's faith, in time, showed him the same answer. When I look at the cross, I don't see a remote and righteous God, using pain to reform a sinful world. Nor do I see a disembodied spirit, dismissing the physical world as unimportant. I see Jesus naked, bleeding, gasping, bearing not only terrible physical pain, but the anguish of bringing sorrow to those who loved Him and the spiritual desolation of separation from God.

What kind of pain could ever come to me that Jesus does not know? A nine-year-old boy named Darrell said it best. I heard his words from Erva Merow, a hospital volunteer in Kenosha, Wisconsin.

All Erva could see of little Darrell Truax were his lips and one blistered cheek; the rest of his body was wrapped in layer upon layer of sterile gauze. The fire that had burned him so terribly had taken the lives of four of his family members.

The magnitude of his suffering kept most visitors away from Darrell's room. Even Erva had to escape when the nurses came to turn him. From far down the corridor, she could hear his screams as his seared flesh was touched. One day another patient called out to her: "How can God do this to an innocent child?"

"Don't say anything against God!" Erva heard Darrell's voice ring out. "When it hurts, God cries with me."

THE GREATEST HEALER OF ALL

by Bethany Withrow

All night the pounding of my heart kept me drifting in and out of sleep. Now, on a frosty December morning in 1994, I pulled myself from underneath the warm blankets with great difficulty. Every day, it seemed, I awakened more exhausted than the day before.

Eight years earlier, at seventeen, I had been diagnosed with lupus erythematosus, a degenerative systemic condition that produces a range of debilitating, sometimes mysterious symptoms, including arthritis. For months I had been battling a severe flare-up that had kept me prisoner in my house—except for stays in the hospital when I had fevers as high as 106 degrees. As a result of steroid drugs, I developed diabetes. Today I felt worse than I had in months.

Even breathing was painful. But something stranger was happening. When I touched my face, it felt unusual. I hobbled to the bathroom and sought my reflection in the mirror. Staring back at me was a face I hardly recognized. It was horribly swollen and my left eye drooped.

"Butch!" I called to my husband. He took one look at me and ran for the phone. "I'm calling the doctor."

Dr. Alexander told him to bring me right over. My husband had been by my side through many lupus crises, so to see him this unnerved scared me. I began to worry that I had suffered a stroke. Then in the living room, as I struggled with my coat, a flash of brown through the window caught my eye. There in our wooded yard stood a baby white-tailed deer all alone. *How strange that he came this close*, I thought. Our gazes met and lingered, and I began to feel calm. I love animals. Suddenly, with a graceful little jump, he was gone. But a small measure of that calmness stayed with me.

We were almost out the door when my mom called from Wichita, Kansas, to check on me. I could tell how worried she was. When I was little, Mom used to say she asked God for a "hedge of angels" to protect her children. I reminded her to ask God to keep His angels close to me today.

Lupus is a disease of many guises, and Dr. Alexander couldn't determine what was wrong with me or how to treat it. He took X-rays and drew blood, then sent me home to rest. "Keep still and call me immediately if you get worse, Beth," he said. I knew he was trying to spare me another traumatic hospital stay. Unless my condition was life threatening, I wanted to be at home.

In the car I studied Butch. I knew he hated leaving me to go in to work. He walked me inside the house and made sure I was comfortable on the couch. Then, as he leaned over to kiss me, I felt a tear fall on my brow. "Don't worry," I whispered. "I'm going to be all right."

But the symptoms worsened. I tossed and turned on the couch, my heart thundering. Late in the day I finally tried calling Dr. Alexander but couldn't reach him. I was getting weaker. I talked to Mom again and she said she and her friends at church were praying for me for all they were worth. After we hung up, Mom was so worried she called my father, who lives nearby. He came over to check on me and wasted no time getting me to the hospital.

By midnight I was once again in intensive care, hooked up to oxygen and a slew of beeping, blinking monitors. Butch had taken up his familiar position in a recliner by my bed, while doctors and nurses paraded in and out of my room. Eventually, around 3:30 in the morning, the traffic slowed. Butch nodded off while holding my hand, and I thought I was falling asleep too. Then I realized something altogether different was happening to me, something both wondrous and fantastic.

I drifted in a smoky grayness, not quite floating and not quite walking. I was free of all the medical equipment I had been tethered to moments before. I traveled down an extended passageway. It felt like being inside a telescope; in the dim distance I discerned a glow. With amazement I realized I was no longer in pain. I moved effortlessly toward a radiant, golden light. As I drew closer, I noticed a beautiful figure within the light, standing with outstretched arms. Indescribable peace flooded my senses; the feeling expanded the closer I came to the figure emanating from the light.

All at once I knew I was in the presence of the Son of God. Angels were everywhere, flying to and fro as they hastened to do the Lord's work, each encircled in its own golden bubble of light. The flowing gowns of the angels were translucent and their features were serene, noble and wise.

I was aware of Jesus communicating directly with me, though no words were uttered. His language flowed through me. He told me not to be afraid, that He wasn't ready for me yet, that I would be going back: There are still things for you to do and songs for you to sing. An overpowering sensation of being loved seized me. I felt a joy I had never felt before—the full experience of Christ's love for me.

Suddenly, as if a curtain had been drawn back, I found myself amidst breathtaking surroundings: magnificent mountains, rolling pastures and singing brooks. I saw a distant red barn and I was happy because I knew this meant there were animals in heaven. I thought of the baby deer I had seen that morning and all the animals I loved.

I noticed a couple standing behind Jesus, and angels hovering and singing above them. I recognized my grandmother, who, before she had died the previous year, had been doubled over with osteoporosis. Now she stood straight and tall, holding the hand of my granddaddy. He died long before I was born but I had seen many pictures of him. In his free hand he held a bowl.

I knew what it contained. Mama loved to tell about her daddy's prowess in the kitchen. Saturdays were special. That's when Granddaddy reveled in making his special chili, full of secret, savory ingredients. That bowl contained Granddaddy's Saturday-night chili, and far from seeming irrelevant or bizarre, this fantastic detail reassured me that my grandparents were happy, together again in their love, and that heaven was a place God has made for each of us.

Then Jesus was communicating with me again. "I have given you a special husband, and I have given him strength so he can care for you." I was always aware that Butch was unique; now the words of Jesus filled me with pride and gratitude.

He reminded me once more that there was much left for me to do; then I was zooming backwards through the telescopic passageway as if time had been reversed. Almost instantly I was in my hospital bed again, reattached to the monitors and oxygen. But I was not disappointed. I was thankful and brimming with joy.

Immediately I wanted to tell Butch all about my amazing experience, but he was sleeping so peacefully, I did not have the heart to disturb him. I wondered why the monitors hadn't sounded an alarm while I was gone. My journey had seemed to last a long while. God's time, though, is different; what feels to us like hours may be only a blink of the eye in heaven.

For the first time since returning, I looked around the room, and there they were: angels, angels everywhere, flickering like candlelight, hovering protectively around us like a hedge—a hedge of angels.

No one sleeps late in the hospital. Soon the nurses and doctors were busy, and Butch woke up. I told him my experience and he listened intently, stroking my hand, never doubting for a moment that what had happened to me was real.

All that day things looked markedly different, as if a bit of the light I had seen now touched and infused everyone and everything I encountered. I continued to sense the presence of heavenly beings in my room. Even Butch seemed to have an angelic glow about him.

The doctors were amazed to see that the swelling in my face had gone down and the position of my eye was back to normal. They continued running tests for the next few days, including an MRI. When they slipped me into the cylinder for that test, it was like being back in the heavenly passageway, and again I saw the angels. In the waiting room before the test, a frightened little boy was waiting his turn. I saw an angel hovering over him. I told him what I saw, and he became calm.

At last Dr. Alexander said I could go home. "All we know, Beth," he reported, "is that you suffered a major lupus flare-up and now you're getting better. But you were very, very sick." Then, smiling, he said, "Don't scare me like that again!"

I don't want to scare anybody because I know from my journey that there is nothing to fear when we are with God.

Nothing about life has been the same for me since I saw the angels. I no longer have to take insulin; my fever is gone; my heart beats normally. I still have lupus and I get sick, but it is not as bad or as terrifying as before. Now I have a continual sense of life's secret beauty. I know that God protects us and loves us at all times. Full awareness of that love is the greatest healer of all.

OUR TASK IS SIMPLE

by Marilyn Morgan King

My loss of vision came on gradually, until one day I picked up a book I'd been reading just the day before and found that no matter how close I held it, I couldn't read it! An eye exam showed that glasses would no longer correct the problem; I needed an operation. Yet there was also a slight risk that I could lose my sight in the surgery.

"Oh, God," I prayed, "don't let me fall into darkness!" Then I thought about Jesus healing the man born blind (John 9:1–12), and I was startled to see something in this miracle I hadn't seen before. The spittle and the clay and the washing in the pool were only for the sake of the Pharisees. These were not the real healing tools. The blind man was healed because Christ gave him His own inexhaustible light!

I carried this new awareness into the operating room with me. Awake during the surgery, with one eye covered and the other anesthetized, I could see only light and shadows. Recalling Jesus' words before the blind man's healing, I focused on the blurred light above the table while silently repeating the name of Jesus. As these two things steadied my pounding heart, I became keenly aware of a healing presence in the room—a bright and shining presence that would not let me fall into darkness.

My eye surgery is over, and I can *see* again. Thanks be to God! I'm enjoying so much the *beauty* of clean, clear colors. Pages of books are brighter, my daughter Karen's outfit today was a lovely shade of blue instead of the muddy green I'd thought before, and my walls are transformed from a dullish yellow to a soft, clear white. Best of all, I can *read* again.

Though scalpel and stitches and other surgical tools were used, I believe they were only for the sake of the Pharisee in me. Whether the need is for healing of physical, mental or spiritual blindness, our task is simple: Focus on the light of Christ, trusting that He will not let us fall into darkness.

MY HEAVEN HERE ON EARTH

by Victoria Baker

I was nervous the day we drove from my home to the Work Release Center in Charleston, West Virginia. "It's not too late to change your mind," my husband Don said. He hadn't wanted us to come, didn't believe I should meet the man whose image had haunted me for a dozen years. He had tried to dissuade me from the moment I mentioned the visit, but I was resolute. If I was going to live, truly live, I had to see James Whitsett again face-to-face.

Twelve years earlier, on a wintry evening in 1982, I was parking my car near Don's apartment on Huntington's South Side. Back then Don was my fiancé and he had invited me over for dinner. I closed the car door and took a few steps. Abruptly someone grabbed me, pinned my hands behind my back and threw me to the icy pavement. I looked up and saw a pair of wild, drug-crazed eyes.

The man yanked my hair and punched my face. I tried to scream, but he clamped his hand on my bloody mouth, silencing me. Angry, frightened, I bit his hand and he howled in pain.

"Give me your purse," he snarled. I flung it at him, scared for my life. He stuffed it inside his jacket and ran, leaving me bruised and bleeding on the deserted street. I dragged myself to Don's apartment, finding some solace in the knowledge that I could identify the man who had assaulted me.

By the time I married six months later, the bruises and wounds had healed, and James Whitsett, my attacker, had been given a life sentence. But even with him behind bars, I was haunted by fears. I still trembled at the mention of his name. Once at the supermarket I thought I saw him and abandoned my half-filled cart in the middle of an aisle, hurrying out of the store in a panic. Another time I had stopped my car at a crosswalk when a man who looked like him walked by. I felt a surge of anger and for a split second considered gunning the engine and hitting the innocent stranger.

I lived in terror for myself and, after Don and I had children, for our family. I locked all car doors and even double-bolted the front door in our safe neighborhood. Four years after the attack, I was still fighting James Whitsett. Other, graver fears intruded in my life, but they could not erase that one primal fear or relieve me of the image of those eyes. Nothing terrified me more, not even learning in 1986 that I had cancer. The tumor was successfully removed, but the cancer came back. I had more operations and radiation therapy, but the malignancy returned, ever threatening. By 1993, it had spread to my lungs and I was told I had less than a fifty-percent chance of living more than five years.

Around the same time I received word that James Whitsett was up for parole. I told Don, "Do everything you can to make sure he stays in prison." In April I went to Ohio State University Medical Center in Columbus for intensive radiation therapy, requiring a three-day stay in an isolated, cell-like room. While there, I lay on my bed, saying prayers for my health. I saw the radiation as light, spreading through my body. "By his stripes we are healed," I repeated, and I imagined every part of my body touched by the healing blood of Jesus. But I never offered any prayers for the anger and fear that were also riddling my body; I held onto my hatred for the man in another cell.

That summer I was well enough to go with my two eldest sons to church camp. I wanted to savor what time I had left with them. One evening at campfire I closed my eyes and listened to the songs that took me back to my girlhood, when I was trusting and carefree. "Oh, how I love Jesus," we sang, and the words became my prayer. That's the last thing I remembered before I collapsed . . .

I see the sky, beyond the blue, out of reach of the stars. I see my younger brother Rene. He died at twelve, but here he's grown up. He smiles at me and sings. My mother too is here. The last time I saw her, her face and body showed the ravages of cancer, but now she is healthy and happy again. This is heaven. I hear the angels sing, a music more glorious than any I have ever heard before. I am so close to the angels I sing with them, "Oh, how I love Jesus."

Lying on the ground, I feel the hand of God touch the pit of my stomach and move up through my chest and neck with an intense heat. I hear God speak. "Be still," He says. "Now say, 'I am healed.'" I repeat those words, "I am healed. I am healed!" Then I get up and join the dance.

When I opened my eyes I was still on the ground. A friend was standing over me and I told her the good news: "I have seen heaven." I hadn't been praying for healing, I had just been concentrating on God and suddenly I had seen His realm. The door was opened to me and I had seen the beyond.

The first concrete evidence of my physical healing came in the fall when I went back to the OSU Medical Center to have my blood tested. My physician, Dr. Ernest Mazzaferri, was looking for a marker to see if cancer was present. The last time he had run the test, I had had a marker count of around one hundred. This time it was close to five—perfectly normal. "I couldn't believe it," Dr. Mazzaferri said. "I made the lab run the tests twice just to be sure there hadn't been any mistake."

For me the New Year of 1994 felt like the beginning of a new life. I could look ahead to the future with better expectations. But in February, when James Whitsett came up for parole again, I started to revert to that old familiar feeling—fear.

I had been so grateful for my healing, had felt so happy, had trusted

God so completely, that I had almost forgotten my attacker. But now that man was back in my thoughts, spoiling my life. One night at dinner I announced, "I want to see James Whitsett."

Don nearly dropped his fork. "You can't," he said. "I won't let that man hurt you again."

"For as long as I harbor anger against him, I am hurting myself," I explained. "If I can trust God with my health, I have to trust God with this. I don't think I'll be completely well until I see James in person."

Don looked down at his plate, thinking. "Then I'm coming with you," he said.

After calls to the parole officer of the work-release program in Charleston, James agreed to see me, but the woman in charge was deeply suspicious of my motives. "If you attempt to intimidate him or retry him," she said, "the visit will be terminated."

We went into an office and waited. Then the door opened and in walked a thin man wearing a teal sports coat, black trousers and shined shoes. How different he was from the person I saw in my nightmares. He looked smaller, older, a little frightened.

"James," I said, "you look nice."

Self-conscious, he straightened his shirt collar and sat down across from us. "Thank you," he said softly.

Don squeezed my hand. Not sure of what more I was going to say, I leaned forward, looked James in the eye and asked, "Will you forgive me?"

James looked at Don, then back at me. "I tried to convince myself that I was justified in my anger at you," I said, "but it probably made me sick inside."

James listened while I told him about my cancer and the miracle of my cure. I could already see that another miracle was taking place in that room. It was as though the angels were back with me, showing me how to make my heaven here on earth.

James wanted to tell me more about himself, who he was before drugs and alcohol took hold of his life. He pulled two crumpled newspaper clippings from his pocket and handed them to me. I read about a star high school athlete destined for a great future, an All-American basketball player with college scholarship offers. "Kids used to ask me for my autograph," James said. "Then . . . " He fumbled for words. "I'm sorry I hurt you and your family."

We were both silent for a while. Then James said, "May I ask you something? Will God hear my prayers?"

"Absolutely. I believe that God can change you—has changed you. He sure changed me." My anger and fear were gone. I was free.

The next day I went to a bookstore and bought a Bible. I had James Whitsett inscribed in gold on the cover and mailed it to him with some highlighters and a note reading, "Mark whatever speaks to you. Make it personal."

That was two years ago. Today James is out of prison. He is dating a religious woman and has a good job at a Charleston restaurant. Most important, James has become a friend. We talk on the phone every few weeks and we exchange cards and letters. He's even had dinner at my home and traded sports stories with my sons.

That's how deep my healing has been. Nothing this side of heaven could have made me whole.

THE DOCTOR'S NAME?

by Sam Nix

Here in South Korea, where I'm stationed with the United States military, I met Ms. Kyong Cha Lee, a woman who had suffered a terrible loss.

Ms. Lee's house, like many older homes in Korea, is heated by large charcoal briquettes placed under the floor. During a cold spell last spring, this primitive heating system malfunctioned, spreading poisonous carbon monoxide fumes throughout the house, almost killing Ms. Lee.

She lay in the hospital in a coma for days, with her family at her bedside. When she finally awoke, they were too grieved to tell her the extent of her loss. But she astonished them when she said she already knew her two children had been killed in the tragedy. "The doctor told me when he came to look after me," she explained.

"What doctor?" they asked.

"The doctor who prayed by my side and promised that God would watch over me."

They assured her they had seen no such visitor and they had been with her constantly. The physician must have been a dream, they said.

When Ms. Lee was well enough to go home, she was making her way out of the hospital when she caught sight of a portrait in the lobby. "There," she said, "that's the doctor who came to my bedside. What is his name?"

"Jesus Christ," came the answer.

And that's the story I heard from Ms. Lee at a retreat recently. She was there with a number of others who, like her, were new in the Christian faith.

The healing of His seamless dress
Is by our beds of pain;
We touch Him in life's throng and press.
And we are whole again.

—JOHN GREENLEAF WHITTIER

IT WAS JESUS, GAZING DOWN

by Roberta Messner

Driving down East Pea Ridge Road on a chilly evening last February, I squinted into the darkness, trying to ignore the throbbing pain behind my left eye. I was on my way home from an all-day conference that had been billed as a booster shot for flagging faith. I'd needed it in the worst possible way. Chronic illness had affected every area of my life. My work as a nurse once brought great joy; now just getting through my shift was a daily battle. Doctors' bills ate up my savings. Too often I cancelled meetings with friends when pain struck. Folks eventually stopped making plans with me.

The worst part was the emptiness I felt, as if illness had blotted out my true self. I couldn't sense God anymore. Even getting down on my knees and praying out loud didn't seem to help. I tried writing out my prayers in a journal. But my confused ramblings looked so ugly in contrast to the pretty rose-sprigged pages that I tore out all my entries and ripped them to pieces.

The conference had been my last hope, but a latecomer had squeezed into my row, hefting a backpack loaded with books. The backpack hit me square in the eye, giving me a blinding headache. I rushed from the building to my car, eager to get home to an ice bag and my bed.

I was headed down East Pea Ridge Road when I heard a sickening thump, followed immediately by a yelp of pain. My foot slammed down on the brake pedal. I looked frantically over my shoulder and saw a mass of fur on the road. "Oh no!" I cried. I'd hit a dog!

I jumped out of the car and hurried through a group of onlookers. I dropped to my knees on the road next to the dog and stroked her soft fur. She was badly hurt, bleeding profusely and barely moving. "Jesus. Oh, Jesus," was all I could say. But I knew God wasn't listening. How could something like this have happened if he were?

A young man crouched beside me. "I'm a vet's assistant," he said. "Looks like she's got a broken hip. Maybe some internal injuries. You could take her to the animal ER, but they'll probably end up putting her to sleep." He looked over the dog while rubbing her ear. "No collar. Most likely a stray."

"She can't die!" I said helplessly. Just as the words left my lips, an inner voice took command: *Trust me, Roberta. Let me take care of everything.*

"If you want," the man said, "I'll take her to the ER in my car. You can follow."

I ran to my trunk and took out a thick antique rug I'd bought recently. The man and I lifted the dog onto it. By the time we got her loaded into the back of his car, the rug was soaked through with blood.

I followed close behind during the twenty-mile trip to the animal ER. My head still pounded, but that didn't seem important anymore. Nothing mattered except saving that injured dog. Yet doubts crowded out my prayers. *What does God care about a dog? What does God care about you? You're just one person in a world teeming with people in need.* Again the inner voice spoke: *Let me.*

I flew into the parking lot and pulled up next to the man's car. I dashed inside, got to the check-in desk and blurted, "I'm the woman who hit the dog that young man just brought in. Do they think they can save her?" The receptionist avoided my eyes. "Number where you can be reached?" she asked.

I gave her the information, then collapsed into a chair in the corner. Finally someone called my name. I followed a woman to a room with a metal table. On it was the dog, bandaged all over with an IV in one of her front legs. Despite her injuries and the harsh fluorescent light, she looked beautiful—a grayish-brown German shepherd mix. I imagined she was a watchdog for some family. I leaned over and gently kissed the top of her head. "I'm so sorry I hurt you," I whispered. "I didn't mean to. You know that, don't you?" Her eyes remained closed.

It was just one thing after another—my illness; getting smacked by the backpack; hitting this dog. I wished I could help her, but I couldn't even help myself.

Desperate, I cupped the dog's face in my hands and began talking out loud, forgetting about the vet and assistants in the room. "I don't know how to help you," I told the dog. "But I know someone who does. God knows everything about you. He made you. He wants the best for you." My words startled me. They were promises I'd once clung to, my belief in them instilled and nurtured by years of Sunday school, church, Bible reading and prayer. But my faith had been beaten down by illness. A picture formed in my mind. It was Jesus, gazing down at the dog with eyes of such compassion that they took in every cell, every molecule, of her body.

"I have to go home now," I told the dog at last. "But don't worry. God will be with you. He's watching over you as if you're the only dog in the whole world."

"Promise me one thing," I said to the vet. "Don't put her to sleep without calling me." Then I thanked the young man who'd brought the dog in, and left.

When I got home I put an ice bag on my head and fell into bed. I tried to sleep, but two images kept appearing in my mind: the dog bleeding on the road and Jesus gazing down at her in the animal hospital. *Why did You let me hit that dog? Why weren't You watching over me too, Lord?* I felt so lost.

In the darkness and silence of my bedroom, the inner voice answered. *You are never lost, Roberta. Every day, every instant, I watch over you as if you were the only one in the world. I am with you, even in your suffering.*

There in the stillness of the night, that voice seemed to reverberate through my very being. I felt myself relax. My pain subsided, not just the pain in my head but also the pain deep inside me. I drifted off to sleep. The ringing phone woke me in the morning. I picked up the receiver hesitantly. "This is a fine dog you've got here," a male voice said. "You can come pick her up any time." Pick her up? There must have been some mistake. Please don't let them have put her to sleep, I prayed, then got dressed.

At the ER the dog raised her head and greeted me with a bark. She was still bandaged, but the IV was gone.

Again I cupped her face in my hands. "Are you really all right?" She barked once more, a happy, healthy bark that said, "Let's get out of here!" The vet couldn't explain her recovery. "She's one lucky dog," was all he could say.

I took her home and put an ad in the paper. The next morning a man called me. "That dog sounds like our Lucy. She lifted the latch on the storm door and got out the other day. Looks like she wiggled out of her collar too; it's still here on the living room floor. I tell you, we've been worried sick."

We agreed to meet each other later that day. The man was sitting on a concrete bench when I arrived. The dog jumped up and licked his face, her tail a blur. It was his Lucy all right.

Introducing myself, I explained to him about the accident. "I am so sorry. I feel just terrible," I said.

"I'm just relieved she's not lost," he said, rubbing her ears. "The kids haven't stopped crying since she ran off."

He tried to pay me for the vet bill, but I was having none of it. After all, I was feeling restored myself, at least spiritually. And isn't that where true healing always takes place, in the soul rather than the body?

I watched them pull out of the parking lot. Lucy clambered over the backseat and pressed her nose to the rear window. I could swear she was looking right at me. We were both going home.

· PART 5 ·

Glimpses of Jesus
as Guiding Light and Leader

AS AN ADOLESCENT I particularly liked one record album that included this prayer-song by Doris Akers.

> Lead me, guide me, along life's way,
> For if you lead me, I cannot stray.

Of course for Jesus to lead me, I must be willing to follow. "I am the light of the world," he said. "Whoever follows me will never walk in darkness, but will have the light of life" (John 8:12 NIV).

The stories in this section illustrate how Jesus, through his Spirit, has guided the steps of men and women—and one special young boy named Wilson; his mother, Denise Wicks-Harris, tells of his keen awareness of Jesus' call on his life.

In the thoughtful chapter "God Does Speak to Us," Marion Bond West responds to a reader who asks: "Can you tell me how" God speaks to you? Softly and tenderly, she says. May the lessons Marion shares draw you closer to Jesus, who is the Way, the Truth and the Life—as well as the ultimate guiding Light.

AS VIVIDLY AS YOU CAN

by Norman Vincent Peale

Nowhere in any of the four Gospels is there a physical description of Jesus, and I have often wondered why this is so. Here are four devoted followers telling us about the most wonderful Person they ever encountered, and yet they don't tell us what He looked like. Perhaps it doesn't matter; perhaps the words He spoke and the things He did are portrait enough.

My own concept of what Jesus looked like was formed years ago when I was a youngster growing up in Ohio. In Sunday school one day the teacher was telling us about the dangers that closed in on Jesus near the end of His ministry. She said that He was relatively safe in Galilee, but in Jerusalem powerful forces were plotting His death. He knew this, but even so—and here she opened the Bible and read—"He . . . set his face to go to Jerusalem . . ." (Luke 9:51 KJV).

And suddenly I could see Him in my mind. A tall, sun-bronzed figure, lean and hard from tramping those primitive roads. I could see Him striding along followed by His disciples and the surging crowds that sought Him everywhere. There He went, strength and goodness in motion, courage and resoluteness in action, kindness and love personified.

I knew then, even as a small boy, that I wanted to follow Him too. All the happiness, all the usefulness I may have had in life, I think, can be traced back to that moment.

Try to see Him as vividly as you can. Then you'll want to follow too.

Take time to be holy, let him be thy Guide,
And run not before him, whatever betide;
In joy or in sorrow, still follow thy Lord,
And, looking to Jesus, still trust in his Word.
—WILLIAM LONGSTAFF

INSISTENTLY DRAWN TO LOOK

by Elizabeth Rockwood

One summer, some friends of ours sent their daughter Lisa to camp. It was Lisa's first time away from home. As she entered the camp, with her sparkling eyes and honey colored braids, she was the picture of enthusiasm.

However, most unfortunately, it rained during most of the six-week session. The many outdoor activities were constantly being cancelled, and the little campers had to spend many hours in their small, leaky cabins. Although Lisa never complained, it was evident from her long, daily letters that she wished she were home.

Elaine and Dave, her parents, felt it would be best for Lisa to make it through until the camp's end. Nevertheless, they went to visit her one weekend as a way of encouragement.

Afterward, as they drove away, they could see Lisa in their rearview mirror. Bravely, she waved them out of sight, her long, honey-colored braids wet in the falling rain.

The next day Elaine's heart was heavy. While driving to market, she happened to pass a church with a sign out front reading: "Chapel Open for Prayer." Although she had never stopped there before, she parked and went inside.

Kneeling in the quiet, she prayed for Lisa. As she shared her concern with the Lord, she felt insistently drawn to look over her left shoulder. Turning, she saw a bright colored stained glass window. In it, the artist had beautifully depicted Jesus standing in the midst of children. He was gazing down at a little girl. Arms raised, she offered Him a bouquet of wildflowers. She had long, honey colored braids.

Elaine gave a little gasp. The coincidence was startling. Surely the Lord had guided her to the chapel to remind her that Lisa was in His loving care.

THE COUNSELOR

by Gayle Miller

I'm a businesswoman, and I conduct seminars for other businesswomen. So it comes as a surprise to some people that one of the most important furnishings in my office is a picture of Jesus.

The picture came to my husband and me as a gift from a friend some years ago when I was president of Anne Klein II, a manufacturer of designer sportswear.

I unwrapped the package to find a print portraying Jesus sitting next to a businessman at his desk, the two obviously in deep conversation. It was titled "The Counselor."

"Thank you. It's a lovely thought," I told our friend, and put the picture aside. However, every once in a while I picked it up and glanced at it. The more I looked at it, the more I began to be drawn to it. Eventually I hung it in my office on Seventh Avenue in New York's bustling garment district. At first I noticed some of my colleagues looking at it skeptically. It certainly wasn't the kind of picture you'd expect to see in the busy office of a company producing designer clothes.

But soon, I'm sure, it blurred into the background. People in the garment district are more attuned to design sketches and fashion photos on the wall than a religious painting. They move at a fast pace. There are decisions to be made on designs and fabrics, manufacturing problems to iron out, delivery dates to arrange and, at market time, new clothing lines to be presented to retail buyers.

However, in the midst of my hectic pace, from time to time I found myself glancing up at "The Counselor." It became a pleasant respite from the confusion surrounding me.

Then one day that picture took on a new significance. It happened late one hectic afternoon when everything seemed to have gone wrong. I found myself on the phone in a heated argument with a retail buyer. It appeared he wanted to take unfair advantage of us over a merchandise exchange. His voice was strident and my temper rose. As we sparred back and forth, his tone became more demanding and each accusation shot my blood pressure higher.

"Listen—" I found myself beginning to retort with a vengeance. Then I glanced up at "The Counselor." Immediately it seemed as if Christ was reminding me: "Be not hasty in thy spirit to be angry: for anger resteth in the bosom of fools" (Ecclesiastes 7:9 KJV). I caught myself and was silent for a moment.

"Hey, you still there?" snapped the man.

"Yes, I'm here," I said—quietly. "Somehow it seems we've gone off the track. We're not understanding each other." I found myself forcing out the next words: "It could be my fault."

Again there was quiet. Then came his response: "Sorry. . .I think I might be the one who flew off the handle. It's been a lousy day here and, well. . ."

We began talking like two reasonable people and ended up with a mutually satisfactory answer to the problem.

Since then, "The Counselor" has time and again been a graphic reminder of Whom I should look to for direction. That picture has reminded me not to react out of my own emotions but to think of what He would say. To me it personifies His message in Psalm 32:8 (KJV): "I will instruct thee and teach thee in the way which thou shalt go: I will guide thee with mine eye."

I have a partnership with Jesus. And that picture helps to remind me that He is always there to counsel me when I'm overburdened, to guide and direct my thoughts when I'm confused, to inspire me when I'm burned-out and to comfort me when I'm lonely. So wherever I go, whatever office I'm in, "The Counselor" will have a place over my desk.

THEN I REMEMBERED

I woke, weeping, from a dream about a life long ago, when my children were young and I was their gallant knight. But alone in the darkness at 3:47 AM, I was only an old man dreaming of the past.

Then I remembered that Jesus said He would send the Holy Spirit to be with us as Counselor, to teach us and *remind* us of what Jesus had taught (John 14:26). So I prayed, "God, I'm lonely and miserable. My faith has apparently lost its power, and I can't remember what to do!"

The words formed in my mind: *What would you tell someone else to do in this situation, Keith?*

"I'd say something like, 'I too have awakened in the dark, feeling lost many times over the years. And God has always helped me through.'"

What happened? What did He teach you to do?

"Turn on the light and get out of bed. Then do something! Even God would have trouble guiding a stationary object. You've got to be moving to get guidance. So get up."

What next, after you get out of bed?

"Well, I go into the kitchen and brew a cup of herbal tea. Then I sit down at the breakfast table and go through the Twenty-third Psalm, reminding myself that God has helped people for thousands of years—

118 · A CLOSER WALK WITH JESUS

even through 'the valley of the shadow of death.' And then I say a prayer of commitment."

Anything else?

"Well, the rest doesn't sound too spiritual. But I need to let some time pass for God to do His work on my fearful feelings. So if I still can't go to sleep, I may read a novel, the sports section of the paper, a magazine about travel or anything that points me toward the future—where my midnight demons do not live. And by the time I've acknowledged Him as Lord and taken a few small steps out of 'the land of shadows,' I usually even feel some peace."

Let us fix our eyes on Jesus,
the author and perfecter of our faith. . . .

—HEBREWS 12:2 (NIV)

GOD DOES SPEAK TO US

by Marion Bond West

Of course, God doesn't tap you on the shoulder and exhort you like your boss, in deep, commanding tones. No, He makes Himself known in various ways. Here's how I came to learn to make myself available to Him.

I never wanted anything in life but to be a wife and mother. I believed this was my calling. When I married Jerry, it all came true for me. By 1968 I was the mother of two young girls and infant twin boys. All four were active and demanding. Suddenly I was up to my ears in diapers and formula and laundry; some days I was so dragged out I never got out of my bathrobe.

Jerry and I were both believers, and when I got the children dressed and we trooped off to church each Sunday, we looked like a picture-book family. We were, except for me. I was drained—running on empty. I began to resent that Jerry went to work all week to an interesting job with people he enjoyed while I endured daily bedlam at home.

On the morning of March 4, 1972, I told Jerry, "I've got to be alone for a while. Please take the children."

"Sure, sure," he said brightly. "I understand. Maybe it'll cheer you up."

"That's easy for you to say," I said through clenched teeth. Jerry got the message. He quickly collected the children and packed them off outside to the yard. It's fortunate he did or I might have screamed at him. I was screaming inside.

I felt like a failure as a wife, mother and person. I went into the den, shut the door and whimpered, "Help. Lord, please help me. Take over, I can't do it anymore. There's got to be something more for me in life."

I stood stock still. I wasn't absolutely sure what I was doing. But I listened. Oh, how I listened.

And then I began to feel something, a feeling of warmth. I felt a love so intense that it seemed to fill and overflow from me and permeate the den and reverberate throughout the whole house. . . .

I didn't need to hear words; I could sense Jesus saying, *I've waited a long time for you to do this. I'm pleased and I'm going to help you. I love you.* Although I didn't see anything visible, I knew that Jesus was with me now in a way that He'd never been before, and I felt He was smiling. I smiled back. I'd almost forgotten how to smile. I wondered how I had sung "In the Garden," "And He walks with me, and He talks with me, and He tells me I am His own," almost all my life at church and never once heard Him "say" anything to me before.

Shortly after that experience, I began thinking more and more about my writing—maybe I should write a book. The idea kept returning. Could it be that God was instructing me to write a book?

"I can't," I told Him. "I don't have the time or energy or know-how. I have four small children. I can't even spell. You know how tired I am after the children are asleep. My typewriter is ancient. I want to, but . . . . Tell you what, Lord. You know that nice editor lady at Guideposts who writes me the encouraging rejection letters, Dina Donohue? Well, if she were to write in her next letter (if there is another letter), 'Dear Marion' instead of 'Dear Mrs. West,' I'd know You were speaking and telling me to write a book . . . and I'd do it."

A letter from Dina Donohue (another rejection) arrived that week. I was standing at our mailbox waiting and looking for it. I read it still standing by the box: "Dear Marion, I cannot call you Mrs. West any longer, for I know you far too well." I laughed, cried, jumped up and down in the yard and ran around in a joyful circle as my astonished children gaped.

"God wants me to write a book!" I fairly screamed to them and the neighbors. No one in the world, no theology, no argument, no logic could have convinced me that The God of the Universe had not spoken directly to me! It was a long road, but my first book was published four years later.

Sometimes even as I learned to listen for God's voice ("My soul, wait thou only upon God," Psalm 62:5 KJV), there have been long, dark, almost unbearable stretches when He didn't speak—or at least I didn't hear Him. When discouraging silence prevailed, I learned that there were always such verses as John 14:18 (KJV): "I will not leave you comfortless," and Psalm147:3 (RSV): "He heals the brokenhearted," and many more definite promises. I had to choose to stand on them and believe them no matter what—as if they were being written for me today.

Once when I was having trouble connecting with God, I asked Him, "Why is it so difficult?" No answer came. Months passed. One night I picked up a book to get my mind off the threatening depression I sensed I'd be facing the next day. Then five words from *My Utmost for His Highest* by Oswald Chambers seemed suddenly almost to leave the printed page and invade my defeated spirit like a conquering army rushing to the rescue: "All noble things are difficult." I sat straight up in bed reasoning: *If all noble things are difficult. . . then I must be doing something noble!* Almost instantly the suffocating depression was lifting. But then I thought, *Why get so excited over five words? Millions of people read this book.* I tuned this out. *Belief is for those who want to believe,* I had heard from God. I went to sleep savoring, rejoicing in those five words.

Shortly after I began "hearing" from God, Jerry's and my old argument about breakfast resurfaced. Or maybe it was I who argued. Jerry only asked that I cook breakfast, but I hated messing up the kitchen early in the morning. One night after my prayers but before drifting off to sleep, I sensed the words *Cook breakfast for your husband* flashing across my mind.

When I turned to Jerry I saw he was still awake, so I told him, "Jerry, I'm cooking you a good breakfast in the morning." He was so excited that he woke up all during the night wanting to know if it was morning yet. That dutiful obedience put a longed-for new spark in our marriage. Over breakfast Jerry looked at me as if we were dating again. Blessings always follow obedience.

So many times I haven't understood at all why God "told" me to do something, except in retrospect. At another low point in my life God seemed to be telling me to help a quadriplegic: Teach him to paint. "Look," I said, "I can barely paint myself. How can I teach him?" I protested all the way to the hospital where I did volunteer work. When I got to the man's room, he was strapped on a Stryker frame, face down, with his back to me. This is absurd, I thought, but I did as God told me and said to the back of his head, "Hi, would you like to learn to paint?"

"Yep. When do we start?" That was in the days before Joni Eareckson had made mouthpainting a nationally known technique. I had nothing to go on except instructions from God. The young man began to paint marvelous pictures with a brush held in his teeth. They were framed free of charge by a businessman who recognized his talent. An article about him appeared in the paper. He learned to type by tapping keys with a wand held in his teeth, and went on to lead a full life. How could I stay depressed after I had witnessed a young man make a new life for himself like that?

God's voice is gentle, never pushy. Even when He spoke to me years ago as I stood frying chicken for supper and a dangerous situation was at hand, His voice was calm. I kept "hearing," *Go find your boys. Now.* Finally I went, hands still covered in flour, to look for them. I thought, *How silly to stop cooking just to look for the boys.* I found Jan and Jeremy in the washroom. Jeremy was crouched in the dryer with the door shut, wearing a space helmet. Jan was about to blast him off into outer space by pushing the "on" button.

There have been times when I've misunderstood God's messages. But even the biblical Samuel missed God's voice a couple of times. However, Samuel was willing to learn to listen. The third time God spoke to Samuel, he answered, "Speak, Lord, for thy servant hears" (1 Samuel 3:9 RSV). I think God just wants us to be willing to learn to listen and that He is pleased when we fully expect Him to speak. John 10:27 (RSV) says, "My sheep hear my voice, and I know them, and they follow me . . ." and in Isaiah 30:21 (RSV) it says, "And your ears shall hear a word behind you, saying, 'This is the way, walk in it'. . . ." Ezekiel 12:25 (KJV) says, "For I am the Lord: I will speak. . . ." I believe God likes to speak. But there are times when I goof. I blow it. Later, when I realize my mistake, I confess, "I'm sorry, Father. Forgive me. I was wrong."

It's all right, child. I know you want to hear from Me. That's all I want. Keep listening. Expecting Me to speak. Don't tune Me out. You are making remarkable progress. I long to tell you so much more.

"Speak, Lord, for Your servant is listening."

MORNING EPISTLE

by Janet Shaffer

I used to feel cheated when I heard friends say that God talks to them, giving guidance and direction. *What's wrong with me, I wondered, that I could not also hear His voice?*

Then at a retreat I attended last year, one of the speakers told us quite seriously that God writes him a letter each morning. He explained that after his prayers and Bible reading, he takes pen in hand and jots down the first words that come to his mind. "It's as if God were speaking to me personally," he said.

Now, morning after morning, I invite Jesus to write me a letter in my notebook. "Visit Jean," He said recently. And, sure enough, Jean was ill that day. "You've been a little cranky lately," I wrote about myself another morning. "Tell your husband you love him."

How exciting to think about what He might be writing me next.

"DO REMEMBER ME"

by Denise Wicks-Harris

Twilight shadows stole softly across the floor of my new apartment as I nursed my infant son, absorbed in the fresh wonder of motherhood. Long after I finished nursing, I held him close, hearing his tiny breathing, smelling his baby smell. Our small living room turned from mellow to cool dusk. I snapped on the lamp, bathing the room and us in a glow of happiness.

"This is our home, Wilson, cozy and safe," I whispered, kissing his soft cheek. Recently I'd separated from my husband and moved from Philadelphia, Pennsylvania, to Mount Kisco, New York.

At last my life was getting settled. I'd found a job as a domestic where I could keep Wilson with me. Our apartment was in a large complex, convenient to shopping and with wonderful neighbors. There was a big grassy lot and a playground. Important things for Wilson and his older sister Yolaine as they grew.

I was still holding this sweet burden of mine when he fell asleep. As I leaned back to rest, suddenly I jumped. A voice, soft and gentle, said, *You will have Wilson for only a short time. Teach him about God.*

My heart was pounding. "Was that You, Lord?" I asked, knowing it was. Shifting a sleeping Wilson to one arm, I went to the window and pulled the cord on the drapes. Would I see an angel? There was only the dark silhouette of the maple tree blowing in the October wind. I hurried to the phone and called my mother.

Her calm, familiar voice reassured me. "Don't worry," she said. "Short time could mean a normal life span because the Bible says, 'A day with the Lord is as a thousand years.' Perhaps God has a special purpose for Wilson and wants you to start teaching him right away."

Of course! I began singing to him and talking to him of Jesus' love.

When Wilson was two he was diagnosed as having hemophilia. It would be hard and often painful for my son, especially since he was so active. But we could live with it.

Then when Wilson was four I got shattering news. Through an infusion of blood protein, he contracted the virus that causes AIDS. The doctor had tears as he told me. I looked this caring man in the eye and said, "My son will be the one in a million to beat this." The doctor didn't answer, but neither would he dash my hope. We immediately began with the drug AZT, which has prolonged the lives of many AIDS patients.

For five years Wilson continued with his normal routine. Then the virus struck. Still I couldn't believe he would die. I prayed hard.

During the last few months of second grade Wilson began a downslide. He loved school. His teachers were great and wanted him there, despite his physical problems. He was an outgoing child who was popular with all the kids as well.

One day the school nurse called me at my desk where I was a receptionist at Mount Kisco Medical Group. Wilson had had a seizure. He was going down the steps at recess and hit the wall, breaking his glasses. Would I please come right away?

I found him lying on a cot in the nurse's office, his face swollen and bruised. He was dazed, but managed a feeble smile and tried to sit up. He was a fighter. I slipped his broken glasses in my purse, knowing they could easily be fixed and wishing all of life was that simple. "Come on, honey,"

I said, my arm supporting him, "the doctor will adjust your medicine and it will be all right."

And it was. For a little while Wilson was back to his old self, almost. I'd watch him through the bedroom window of our apartment, where kids, just home from school, were gathering. They were skateboarding and after that, chasing one another around the jungle gym. There was a catch in my throat as Wilson drifted to the sidelines and sat lethargically on the grass while Yolaine followed and kept an eye on him. After a while I heard his footsteps, weak and shuffling, on the outside stairs. I opened the door.

"Wilson. . ."

"I'm all right, just tired," he said in his little boy voice that belied man-sized courage. As he reached for a book and slumped on the couch, I wondered if there were any limits to his bravery. There were.

Mid-June came, the last two weeks of school, and Wilson had to drop out. A crushing blow. He was running a high fever that wouldn't break and the doctor had him hospitalized.

Einstein Hospital in New York City's Bronx is an old, plain building fighting its age and looks with fresh paint. Wilson was in the pediatric unit in a small private room with a bed next to a deep-sill window overlooking the street. It had a chair that folded back for me to sleep in at night. I used my vacation and sick time from work to stay with Wilson.

The next day my son was lying weak in bed, having just returned from a bone marrow scan. The doctors still hadn't found the cause of his fever. Fluid from an IV unit was dripping into Wilson's arm. I reached for my worn Bible and opened it to where Jesus gathered the children on his lap. I read to Wilson, picturing those little ones climbing all over Jesus, His strong carpenter's arms holding them protectively and His eyes burning with love. I thought of those hands that healed all who came to Him when He was on earth, and I sent up another prayer.

Then came an ice-cold shock. Wilson looked up at me and said, "I know I'm dying, but I don't want to leave you yet."

I went numb. With all his medical problems—hepatitis, blood transfusions three and four times a week, limbs locking painfully from internal bleeding, seizures—he had never, ever mentioned dying or giving up. Until now. He was a fighter, and it was important that he keep on fighting if he was going to live.

"Honey, you're not dying," I said. "You're sick, but we're going to fight to make you better. You're going to keep on taking your medicine. You'll get out of the hospital and. . ."

I stopped. His eyes, glued to mine, were pleading. Suddenly I saw the depth of his terror, the awful weight of dying. Of leaving me, his family, friends, his room that meant so much to him, going out of his body and moving to an alien place called heaven. Unlike the visits to his uncle in Philadelphia, there would be no phone calls home. Total separation.

I laid the Bible aside and stroked his thin arm. "Jesus loves you, even more than I do," I said. He fell asleep. I sat still in my chair, looking out the window at a lazy summer day. "Jesus," I began, remembering how easily Wilson prayed, about everything small and great, "I can't believe that he's going to die. But if it comes to that, help my son to know that heaven is wonderful like Your Word says. Help him not to be afraid."

Summer passed in a blur of hospital trips, ups and downs, hope and despair. Before I knew it, the nip of fall had arrived and the leaves were flaming . . . then withering brown, then gone, and it was winter. Wilson was now bedridden at home.

As the winter wind beat against our building, I tried to think of a way to make Christmas special for Wilson. My mother had moved in with us so I could still go to work. "How about his own tree in his room?" she suggested. We got a table-sized one because his room was tiny. The lights winked at him all through the long nights when he couldn't sleep.

Christmas Day came. Family arrived and we celebrated. Wilson was propped up on pillows on the pullout sofa, his hand resting on one of his presents. There was a faraway look in his eyes that couldn't be penetrated, not even by the train set we surprised him with, though he managed a smile and ran the train around the track twice. He fell asleep from the effort.

I sank into a chair next to him. From the kitchen came the clatter of pots and pans, and the smells of ham, fried chicken, mashed potatoes and gravy. Wilson opened his eyes and immediately his face searched for mine, as if to confirm that he hadn't left me yet. I finally admitted it. My son was dying.

January 12, a gray, wintry day, I carried Wilson from his bed to the living room sofa. There I bundled him up for this last trip to the hospital. He looked around at each piece of furniture, each picture on the wall, the doorway, the kitchen table and the dishes drying in the sink, soaking himself in memories. "Jesus loves you," I said, praying that Wilson would know it. Really know it.

At the hospital my own strength was about gone, and as day stretched into night I felt strangely numb and detached, almost in shock. Doctors, nurses, family drifted in and out, urging me to sleep, telling me they'd wake me if anything happened— "anything" being the moment of death. The next morning came. Wilson was thirsty, but he couldn't swallow. The soft drink dribbled out of his mouth. As the day progressed he couldn't talk. I remembered a line from his favorite song and could still hear him at church, handsome in his suit, singing for all he was worth: "When I'm sick and can't get well, Lord, remember me . . . Do, Lord, oh do, Lord, oh do remember me, way beyond the blue."

Please, Jesus . . . It was dark again at a quarter to five, and suddenly Wilson became alert, opening his eyes and looking right at me.

"I'm going home, Mom."

How could I explain to him that this was impossible? "Wilson, Mommy can get oxygen for you, but you can't go home with the IV."

"No, Mom. I mean I'm going home to be with Jesus."

Home. He was calling heaven *home*. Gone was his dread of leaving me and all else he knew and felt connected to. Wilson's eyes were now focused beyond me. "Jesus is coming to get me. Okay, Mom?"

Jesus Himself was coming to take Wilson home. "Yes, Wilson," I said. Fifteen minutes ticked by. My son's eyes closed. His breathing grew more labored. Then stopped. The doctor came in, leaned over and checked his pulse.

"He's gone," the doctor said gently, touching me. Involuntarily I screamed and grabbed my son by the shoulders. Wilson opened his eyes and started breathing again, a pleading look on his face, as if to say, "Let me go . . . home."

In my mind I could see Jesus waiting. "It's okay, honey. You can go now. Mommy's all right."

He smiled, stopped breathing and walked home with Jesus.

CHARLIE AT TULIP TIME

by Beth Sweigard

When spring came the year I turned thirty-five, I rejoiced on the day the first nubbins of tulip buds appeared in the beds I had planted. It was time to start looking for Charlie. The next day a full-blown shiny red blossom unfolded, and soon the beds were a riot of color. I waited and watched. Spring faded into summer and tulip time was over. By the time the winds off Puget Sound blew in the chill of autumn, I was crestfallen.

The preceding year, in the spring of 1969, I had met with a small group of women and gone on a secluded retreat in the woods to pray. I had had so much to be thankful for—a new relationship with Jesus and a healing from hyperthyroidism—but I also had prayed about a couple of things that troubled me. I was mourning my German shepherd, Freddie. And as a single woman, I longed for someone to love and care for—to share my life with.

On that retreat, as I walked and prayed quietly, the gentle voice of Jesus played in my mind: I will send you a man named Charlie for your husband. I asked Him when, and I immediately recalled these words from the Song of Solomon: "For lo, the winter is past, the rain is over and gone; The flowers appear on the earth . . ." (2:11–12 KJV).

"What flowers, Lord?" I asked.

When I looked up, the first thing I saw were two bright-red tulips growing alongside the path. I smiled. Charlie would be coming at tulip time.

But after tulip time passed and Charlie had not come, I recalled that Jesus had not said which tulip time. So I spent long hours at my new pastime, painting pictures of Jesus, while I waited for the next tulip time—and Charlie. I knew he would come.

It had been four years since my journey with Jesus had begun. I will never forget that day in 1966 when I dragged myself into my dreary little house and collapsed onto a chair. I had just returned from University Hospital in Seattle, where my bulging eyes and hair loss had been diagnosed as symptoms of hyperthyroidism. I felt and looked hideous, but I had no insurance to pay for the operation I needed. I had been divorced from an abusive alcoholic, and my only support was my old German shepherd Freddie.

I had even begun to contemplate suicide; then the doorbell rang. I opened the door to the smiling face of a young man in a clerical collar. "Who called you?" I asked, halfway between suspicion and disbelief.

The man introduced himself as Pastor Eugene Anderson. "I'm starting a new church in the area," he said. "May I come in?"

When he told me he had just come from La Crosse, Wisconsin, I blurted out, "That's my hometown!" This was unreal! I had moved from there twelve years earlier to take a job in Washington.

By the time he left three hours later, I had forgotten my despair. And even though I hadn't been to church in years, I decided to attend his church the following Sunday.

The church was actually a rented school gymnasium. A few people sat on folding chairs before a makeshift altar on which rested a Bible, a cross and fresh daisies—in two beer glasses! I felt sure that if God was all Pastor Anderson described him to be, He would prefer some proper vases. So when the pastor called on me the next week I said I would like to buy some vases for the altar. He smiled broadly and said, "What we really need is a painting of Jesus. Will you paint one for me?"

"Paint one!" I exclaimed. "I've never painted anything!"

"Think about it," he said.

As he left, the telephone rang. It was a Mrs. Curtis, who said she was a friend of my mother's in Wisconsin. She said that after talking with my mother she had felt a need to telephone and encourage me. I told her about Pastor Anderson's visit and his request. "I've never so much as picked up a brush!" I told her, and we both had a good laugh. Her call did cheer me up, but afterward I didn't give the painting a second thought.

For a year I seldom returned to church. My health worsened. One day I went home from work very ill and sat in the dark thinking about the God I really didn't know. Pastor Anderson had told me Jesus loved me. I wondered. Could He be disappointed that I hadn't tried to paint that picture? It was all so confusing.

At midnight the phone jangled me awake. It was Mrs. Curtis. I hadn't heard from her in months. "Have you started the painting for the church yet?" she asked.

"Did you call just to ask me that?" I exclaimed, incredulous.

She assured me she had and then urged me to get some art supplies the next day. After she hung up I started shaking. How strange she should call the very night the painting had come to mind for the first time in months.

The next day I bought canvas boards, brushes, every kind of paint. I put it all in my back room, then worried over it for the next three months. I couldn't face the empty canvas, but an inner voice kept nagging me.

Finally I gave in. Tentatively I propped a canvas on the card table and picked up an artist's brush for the first time in my life. When I stroked it on the canvas, it looked right. Slowly my brushstrokes became the face of Jesus. If I made a false stroke, instinctively I sensed how to correct it.

A day and a half later I was finished. When I put my brush down, the face of Jesus regarded me calmly. But by then Jesus was not just on the canvas; He had also come into my heart. I had the painting framed and took it to Pastor Anderson to put in his church.

That experience made me want to learn more about Jesus. Through various Bible studies I came to believe that Jesus continues to heal today, so I trusted Him to heal me. Gradually the symptoms of my hyperthyroidism disappeared. Jesus had brought me healing, peace and purpose. And finally a promise of a husband. So I had planted tulips.

But spring, summer, fall and winter came again, the second, third and fourth years, and no Charlie. I worked, prayed and, in my spare time, painted more pictures of Jesus. When I had filled the walls of my little house, I offered my paintings to The Galilean, a local restaurant.

In April of the fifth year, 1974, when I turned thity-nine, my friend Kathy visited me from California. Like me, she was a refugee from a failed marriage. When I mentioned I was still waiting for my Charlie, she exploded: "That's ridiculous! After five years, you have to put him out of your mind. You need to stop waiting and start looking for someone else."

That night I got on my knees in the darkness of my bedroom. "Lord, I've been waiting for Charlie for five years. I know You can bring him to me, but I'm not going to plant any more tulips. When they stop blooming this year, I'm not even going to cry."

Two days later Kathy and I went to a park. As we sat and talked, a dilapidated old car chugged up and stopped. Out stepped the handsomest man I had ever seen.

"Can you give me directions to the freeway?" he asked amiably. "I seem to have taken a wrong turn."

"Oh yes," I replied, nearly breathless. But as soon as I had told him the way, he smiled his thanks and ducked back in his car.

"Sir, wait!" I shouted as he started off. "You have a flat tire!"

"Oh bother," he said. "I don't even have a jack."

I lent him mine. He had the spare on in a jiffy, and after another smiling thank-you, he sped off. I watched in dismay as his car disappeared. I turned to Kathy. "You were asking me what my type is. Well, that's my type."

That Good Friday The Galilean restaurant hosted a Passover supper in a large banquet room. When I walked into the crowded room, there, sitting quietly in a corner with a Bible in his hands, was the flat-tire man. During the service I could think of little other than this handsome man with prematurely gray hair and soft brown eyes. When the service was over I walked over to him. "Hi," I said.

He looked puzzled. "Have we met?"

When I told him about lending him my jack, he said, "Oh yes, that was very kind of you," and abruptly retreated to the men's room.

Four days later he telephoned. Deeply moved by one of my paintings of Jesus, he had persuaded the restaurant owner to give him my number so he could compliment me. We were in the middle of a nice conversation about the painting when he stopped short and asked, "Are you married?"

When I said no, he said, "Neither am I. Would you like to go for a ride?"

"Yes."

"By the way," he added, "I know your name from the paintings. Mine is Chuck."

Chuck? Charles . . . ? Charlie!

After hanging up, I walked out in the sweet spring air to wait for Charlie among the blooming tulips.

We chugged off. He told me he was resuming his pediatrics practice after a leave of absence. When he bumped into Kathy and me at the park, he had just returned from a two-year medical mission on an Indian reservation in Montana. He explained that he had been called to Montana by a vision of Jesus, a vision identical to one of my paintings in The Galilean restaurant.

I smiled, thinking of waiting those five years, trusting that same Jesus to bring me Charlie at tulip time. It was easy to trust Him after the way He had given me His gift of painting and had healed me. I knew then that I could trust Him always.

With a shy smile tugging at his lips as we rode along, Charlie asked, "Do you think we'll be married?"

"Yes," I said.

And we were.

Lead, kindly Light . . .
Keep thou my feet: I do not ask to see
The distant scene; one step enough for me.

—JOHN HENRY NEWMAN

A PAINTER'S JOURNEY

by Warner Sallman

Many times I have been asked how I happened to paint the *Head of Christ* that has received such wide circulation since it appeared as a painting in 1940.

"Did you have a vision beforehand?" they ask.

"Did you feel Christ's presence?"

"Did you have some kind of religious experience?"

The answer is yes to all these questions, but the real story behind the picture begins with a change that took place in my life shortly after my wedding.

When I married Ruth Anderson, an attractive and dedicated choir member and organist, in May 1916, I was twenty-four years old, was employed as an artist in the field of men's fashions and was prospering financially. In all, it seemed like a cloudless sky, yet storm clouds already were forming below the horizon.

Years before, I had had a tumor in my shoulder, but a surgeon had removed it and apparently it was healed. Then came a major complication in the same area. By the following spring—1917—the pain was acute. I went to several doctors and took various treatments; still the affliction grew worse. Finally I consulted a specialist who made extensive tests.

"You're pretty sick, my boy," he said kindly.

"Tell me the whole truth, doctor," I replied. "I ought to know what's wrong with me."

"You have tuberculosis of the lymph glands," he continued. "I recommend surgery." He hesitated a moment, took my arm, then continued, "Otherwise I cannot give you much hope beyond three months."

The physician's words jolted me severely. I left his office in a daze, and with uncertain steps made my way to a streetcar. On the car I moved up until I was close to the motorman, feeling some protection in his presence. It gave me an opportunity to do a little thinking.

"What shall I do?" I asked myself. "Shall I tell Ruth the whole truth, or conceal what the doctor said until after the baby is born?" It was July, and our first little one was due in September. I feared the revelation would so upset her that serious complications might develop.

I prayed for guidance, and I believed God was directly speaking to me when the conviction suddenly came over me that "Ruth is brave, has a deep faith, and can take it. I'll tell her all."

This I did, not minimizing the "three months to live." Ruth received my words with utmost calm . . . A feeling came over me that she was like a rock—and that through her the Lord would guide us aright.

"Let God's peace come into your heart, Warner," she told me, putting her arms around my neck and looking squarely into my face, her eyes aglow with love. "We'll pray and whatever is God's will for us, we gladly will do it. In three months we can do a lot for Him: and if it be His will to spare our life together for a longer period, we will thank Him for it and go ahead serving Him."

I do not remember the words we used in our prayer together, but I do know we did not ask for a longer life span. We only asked God to guide and bless us and use us. The heart of our prayer was a plea reminiscent of our Savior's in Gethsemane: "Dear Lord, we pray that Thy will be our will, and that in all ways Thy will be done."

In no manner did we forego medical or surgical help, but we felt that if the latter was to be for me, God would make it known. We continued the medical treatments as before, but no revelation came regarding the proposed surgery.

However, something else did happen: by the alchemy of nature or in the Providence of God, the pain gradually grew less, and there were signs of amelioration of the disease. It took months, but complete healing finally took place. We do not minimize the powerful influence of mind over matter—we implicitly believe the Lord can and does heal.

What better proof can there be than that the predicted three months have stretched into more than forty busy, fruitful and happy years—with the added blessing of three sons born to our union.

The important part of this experience is not that I was healed, but that I learned an exciting and dynamic principle: when we turn our lives over to God, without reservation, He can and will do remarkable things through us.

It was this personal philosophy that made it possible for me to draw the *Head of Christ*. It began as an assignment from a small Christian youth publication in January 1924, for a cover design. I thought to do the face of Christ. My first attempts were all wrong. Finally there were only twenty-four hours until delivery date. I tried again and again the preceding evening, but the impressions that came to my mind were futile. I felt disturbed and frustrated.

I went to bed at midnight, restless in spirit, but did ask God once more to give me the vision I needed. Suddenly about two o'clock I came out of my fitful attempts at sleep with a clear, beautiful image of the *Head of Christ* startlingly vivid in my mind. I hastened to my attic studio to record it. I made a thumbnail sketch, working as fast as I could in order that the details of the dream might be captured before fading out of my mind. Next morning I made a charcoal drawing from it.

This *Head of Christ* hardly caused a ripple of comment when it first appeared. But in 1940 I made an oil painting of the "Head" and, in the years since, its distribution has attained phenomenal proportions. Yet I always think of the portrayal as something God did—through me.

For Ruth and I believe that as disciples of Christ our task is primarily seed-sowing of good deeds, good thoughts and good purposes.

Yet we are human enough to enjoy hearing or knowing of results—often strange and unpredictable—accompanying our labors. For instance, there was an incident in Los Angeles. A robber rang the doorbell to an apartment. When the lady opened the door he thrust a revolver in her face and snapped, "This is a holdup. Give me your money and jewelry!"

Just then he looked up and saw behind the woman a large picture on the wall. It was the *Head of Christ.* For a moment he seemed to freeze. Slowly he lowered his gun.

"I can't do it, lady," he gasped, "not in front of that picture." And he turned and ran down the stairs.

· PART 6 ·

Glimpses of Jesus as Giver of Life

IN TWO DIFFERENT GOSPEL STORIES, Jesus called Himself "the life" (John 11:25; 14:6). And in 1 John 5:12 (NIV) the apostle says that anyone "who has the Son has life." On one level this refers to eternal life, beyond the grave. But it also reminds us that our life here and now is God's gift through Christ: "I am come that they might have life, and that they might have it more abundantly" (John 10:10 KJV).

I especially like the first story in this section, which is reminiscent of a biblical miracle, the raising of Jarius' daughter. "Once upon a time, in a kingdom very near," little Rachel Gibson woke up.

"The Incredible Rescue" and "The Unseen Visitor" show Jesus dramatically present, averting physical death in life-threatening accidents. Several stories portray Jesus' power to infuse life into seemingly desperate situations. And Ruth Vaughn reminds us that sometimes the choice is our own: to choose Life in the face of death and then let Jesus surprise us with His grace.

MY FAIRY-TALE PRINCESS

by Nancy Barrett Gibson

Once upon a time, in a kingdom far away . . ."

At bedtime my seven-year-old daughter Rachel had asked again for the story of *Sleeping Beauty*. She pulled the covers to her chin, blue eyes dancing in anticipation of the familiar tale . . . the old hag luring the princess to the tower, the seemingly fatal wound, the deathlike sleep, the wonderful awakening at the kiss of the handsome prince.

What was the story's strange appeal for Rachel, I wondered, as I turned the well-thumbed pages. Several times she'd even got her ten-year-old sister Kimberlee and me to dress up and act out the parts. Rachel was always the sleeping princess, shoulder-length brown hair haloed on the pillow. Kimberlee, in the crown from her ballet costume, would be the handsome prince. Which left me swathed in black as the ugly hag.

Hag, I often thought, was an appropriate role. As a single parent, holding down two teaching jobs while working for a master's degree in English, I was cross and tired much of the time. Yet that night as I closed the book, my feelings were of gratitude. For my children, for the church that had become our larger family, for the weekend starting tomorrow . . .

I closed the bedroom door and switched on the vacuum. If I did the cleaning tonight I could take the girls to the park after school tomorrow. Friday was the one day we could enjoy the luxury of a late suppertime.

Which is why it was nearly six o'clock next evening, dusk already gathering, when we headed home from a carefree afternoon of trees, swings and creek mud. Rachel had invited a friend along, so I had three children in tow as we approached busy four-lane Abrams Street in front of our apartment.

At the curb I stopped to take the girls' hands, Kimberlee on my right, Rachel's friend on my left, Rachel—I thought—holding *her* hand.

Halfway across we stopped again to let a car go past. That is, three of us stopped. Rachel, eager, irrepressible Rachel, did not. In the twilight I saw a blur of white legs streaking right into the path of the oncoming car. In the few seconds unwinding in the eerie slow-motion clarity of shock, I saw her face blanch with fear and indecision as she looked back helplessly wide blue eyes asking whether to turn around or race for the curb.

Equally helpless, I could only shriek, "Rachel! Rachel! Rachel!" as if my cry could stay the onslaught of metal against flesh.

I heard the impact, saw my daughter's body bounce and scrape like a rag doll in a macabre dance for forty feet beyond the screeching machine. I heard screams and realized they were mine. Rachel herself lay silent, so still in her cupped fetal position that as I knelt beside her it seemed impossible this quiet form had ever held the bubbling life that was my seven-year-old.

People were gathering, sirens, police, an ambulance. Paramedics strapped the limp body onto a stretcher while I clung numbly to a single word one of them had spoken. Alive. Rachel was still alive.

Outside the hospital emergency room, Kimberlee and I were joined by friends from church; as the long night passed, their arms and their prayers surrounded us.

Rachel was transferred to the intensive care unit, where I was permitted to maintain a vigil at her side—though in her deep coma, I was told, she could not be aware of my presence. I tried to draw comfort from the fact that X-rays showed no broken bones. Surely this was a miracle almost as great as the fact that she was alive.

The neurosurgeon, however, shook his head. No broken bones meant only that her brain had absorbed the impact. It was possible, he went on, that Rachel would remain in a permanent vegetative state.

Sitting at her bedside, gazing at her unmoving form as twenty-four, then thirty, then thirty-six hours passed, I wondered if death could be harder to bear than this frozen life. To all outward appearances the bright, outgoing little girl I loved was dead already, her skin with a waxlike pallor, hair lying just as I had combed it on the pillow . . .

Suddenly my mind was racing—I had seen all this before: our little dress-up play! Rachel as Sleeping Beauty, motionless, seemingly lifeless, Rachel asking to hear one fairy tale over and over. Suppose her insistence on this particular story had been more than chance.

I decided to treat her as alive and aware! On my way to visit the house where friends were looking after Kimberlee, I stopped by our apartment to pick up that dog-eared copy of *Sleeping Beauty.* As I did, my eye fell on another of Rachel's favorite books, a child's paperback about Jesus raising from the dead the little daughter of Jairus. "The Sleeping Beauty story from the Bible," Rachel always called it.

I turned the pages, lingering over Jesus' words to that mourning throng: "The little girl is not dead, only sleeping."

"The little girl is not dead," I whispered.

Clutching the two books, I returned to the hospital, to read to the still form on the bed as Sunday afternoon passed.

Sunday evening. Forty-eight hours since the accident: no change in Rachel's condition. All night I continued to read and talk to her as though she understood.

Monday. There was a subtle change in the nurses' manner. They no longer rushed eagerly to Rachel's chart for signs of progress. Even the most cheerful and optimistic of them seemed now to accept the coma as irreversible.

Monday night. I went home for a few hours' sleep while friends kept up the prayer vigil they had not for one hour relaxed. Tuesday morning I was back, resuming the reading to the unresponding form beside me.

Tuesday afternoon. For the twentieth time I picked up the paperback about Jairus' daughter. "The little girl is not dead," I read aloud, "only sleeping."

From the bed at my elbow came a rasping, halting voice. Like a 45-rpm record playing at 33, Rachel's lips were forming words: "The li-it-tle gi-irl is not de-ad, on-ly sl-ee-ping."

I stared at the motionless figure on the bed, hardly believing what my ears had heard. But I had heard—heard the very words of Jesus coming from my daughter's mouth.

That night Rachel sat partway up and opened her eyes. As yet she had not recognized anyone, but her doctors were jubilant. The following morning she focused her eyes directly on me and whispered the word mommy. Later that same day she recognized Kimberlee.

Small gains continued throughout the next twenty-four hours, and on Friday, one week after the accident, I took her home. The rest of her recovery was rapid and total, with the neurosurgeon himself using the word *miracle*. Rachel resumed her sunny, buoyant lifestyle—complete even to her favorite bedtime story: "Once upon a time, in a kingdom—"

Not "far away." Not far away at all. "Once upon a time, in a kingdom very near . . ."

THE INCREDIBLE RESCUE

by Robert Bowden

I'm a carpenter, an ordinary man who works hard with his hands. I say this because the experience I'm going to tell you about is a strange one, and I want you to know I'm not the kind of man to go around making up outlandish stories.

The winter of 1971 was a tough one for the building trades in Monmouth County, New Jersey, where my family lived. I write country-western music on the side and play the guitar and sing, so I was able to pick up a few jobs on weekends, but not enough to support my wife and three kids.

Then, just before Christmas, I landed my first solid job in months, on the nuclear power plant that was under construction at Salem, New Jersey, 129 miles from our home in Oakhurst. I was grateful for the work, even though it meant I had to live at a motel in Salem and only got home to see my family on weekends.

The nuclear plant was a massive project, involving more than four thousand men. I was on the crew building the huge, two hunderd-fify-foot cooling towers, like the ones at Three Mile Island in Pennsylvania. My particular job was to erect the work platforms and the wooden forms—plywood sheets nailed to heavy frames—into which the concrete for the thick tower walls was poured.

All my working life I was used to heights, but climbing the steel to the tops of those towers, as high as a twenty-story building, made me nervous. In fact, the whole job made me nervous. On such a vast project there often are lots of injuries. Every day we heard stories of men losing fingers and toes and even arms and legs.

One day in February, about three months into the job, I sat eating breakfast in the motel luncheonette with my buddy John. "Hey, Bob," he said, "you know the motel manager's wife, Mrs. Schmidt? Well, I was passing the office late last night and I heard her crying. I guess business is pretty bad . . ."

"Yeah, well, we all have problems," I replied. "Hey, we gotta get going."

John was silent as we drove to the work site. It was a clear, sunny day but bitterly cold. I was glad I'd be working inside the file tower, fairly close to the bottom, out of the wind, stripping the forms off the hardened walls.

Before I had been at the site ten minutes, the cold was numbing my fingers. High above, sunlight streamed through the circular mouth of the tower. Around me, in the freezing semitwilight at the bottom, there was bedlam as workers swarmed over the scaffolding. From the unfinished floors, a bristling bed of upright steel construction rods protruded.

I grabbed a hammer and a stripping crowbar and paused, looking up at the platform where I'd be working, thirty-five feet above the floor.

"Hey, Jake!" I called to the foreman, my breath steaming the frigid air. "You only got one plank on that platform!"

"It's all right, Bob," he said, trotting over. "If we put up another plank, you won't have room to pull the forms away from the wall. Just be careful."

"Okay," I replied, but I was doubtful; an eight-inch wide board isn't much to stand on.

I climbed up and began prying the forms loose. It was slow and hard, working so close to the wall on that shaky plank, and the plywood forms were heavy and awkward to handle.

By ten o'clock I had managed to get one off. I paused to warm my numbed hands. Down below, I could see my coworkers picking their way through the forest of upright steel rods. Nasty things. They were for reinforcing the floor; each one was five-eighths of an inch thick, and they varied in height from one to three feet. Their tips were flat. All the same, I had seen a fellow worker impaled on such rods about two years before. All it took was one careless move . . .

I began prying the second form loose. It wouldn't budge; it was stuck to the concrete. I pulled harder. Suddenly the crowbar slipped, throwing me off balance. I plunged forward toward the foot-wide opening where the other plank ordinarily would have been. I knew I was falling. Fear tore through me. I cried out, "God, help me!"

Then, incredibly, it happened. The wooden form and the gray wall of the tower vanished in a blaze of brilliant white light. In the middle of that beautiful, clear light, yet not part of it, stood a Man. He was dressed in a white robe made of some kind of silky cloth. There was a rope around His waist and sandals on His feet. His head was covered by a hood that appeared to be part of the robe. Framing the Man's face, and just visible under the hood, was dark brown, shoulder-length hair. He had a beard with a small part in the middle. His dark brown eyes were commanding but kindly.

Then He spoke. The voice was not in my head, but a real, external voice, beautiful and deep, and it seemed to echo. There is a verse in the Bible that reminds me of it: ". . . and His voice was like the sound of many waters" (Revelation 1:15 RSV).

As long as I live, I will never forget His words: "Son, I am going to save you. Just trust in Me. Don't fight Me."

Then He vanished. And I was falling, plunging face down toward those upright steel rods, each one a dagger.

Strangely, all fear had left me. As my body hurtled down toward death, I thought: *Should I try to save myself somehow? Is there anything I can grab . . . ?* There was nothing.

Don't fight Me, the Man's voice echoed through my mind. I abandoned myself to whatever might happen.

Suddenly, I felt some kind of Power turn my body. Now I was no longer falling face down but sideways, rigidly, like a ruler on edge.

I slammed down between the steel rods. My back grazed the concrete floor, then I was jerked up as if on a giant string, bouncing crazily. Then everything was still.

Everybody came running. "Oh, my God! My God!" Jake kept saying.

"He landed on the rods—they're clean through him!" someone cried.

"I can't look! I'm gonna be sick!" somebody else said.

"No . . . no . . . I'm all right," I gasped. "Cut . . . my belt . . ."

A couple of guys rushed in to cut my belt. Suddenly I could breathe again.

"Good God!" Jake said. "I've never seen anything like this. How come those rods didn't go through him?"

My plummeting body had passed between the rods. The belt loop on my pants had snagged the tip of the tallest rod, about three feet above the floor. Miraculously, the loop held, breaking the force of my fall. Except for grazing my lower back on the concrete, I was suspended above the other rods.

Gently my coworkers lifted me off the rods and laid me on the floor. They gasped in shocked surprise when, a few seconds later, I stood up.

"I don't believe it!" one of the guys said. "He should be dead, but he's standing here!"

"Bob, the Lord was with you today," Jake said, "or this never could have happened!"

"That's right, Jake," I said fervently, "the One Who saved me was Jesus Christ. He gets the credit!" I was about to tell them what I had seen, but something stopped me. I figured they'd never believe me, in spite of the miracle they had just witnessed.

At the hospital, X-rays revealed no broken bones. My only injury was a large bruise on my lower back, where it had hit the floor. The doctor prescribed muscle relaxants and sent me home.

Back at the motel, Mrs. Schmidt was already running a hot tub for me. She had heard the news. "You sure you're all right, Mr. Bowden?" she asked, concern etched on her careworn face.

"Just a little woozy from the pills," I replied, sinking down into a chair.

"Well, don't you try going out for supper," she said. "I'll bring you a nice home-cooked meal. You called home yet?"

I told her I hadn't but would, and I thanked her for her concern. Then I remembered John telling me that he had heard her crying, and I felt a pang of remorse at my indifference . . .

The next morning John was surprised to see me at breakfast.

"You're not going in today, old buddy, are you?" he asked.

"Sure," I replied, munching a piece of toast. "I'm okay."

"God was really with you yesterday, Bob," he said, studying me.

I looked back at him, and decided to tell him the truth. "John, just as I fell off that scaffold I saw Jesus Christ."

He slowly lowered his cup and looked away. "That's impossible."

"No," I replied firmly, "it's not impossible. I saw Him, and He saved my life." Then I told him about the vision.

"Bob," he said, after I had finished, "it's not that I doubt your word . . . but I still think it's impossible. Still, you're here today, alive and healthy . . . so maybe it's not so impossible."

All that day I found myself wondering why the Lord had shown Himself to me, and had saved me. *Why had I been singled out for a mira-*

cle? Did the Lord want me to do some great Work in the world? How could I? I was just an ordinary workingman . . .

You can be kind, a voice seemed to say in my heart—and so that night I sought out Mrs. Schmidt to thank her for taking such good care of me the night before, and to chat with her for a while.

I'm still a carpenter, and I still write songs and play and sing. If God has a big job for me, it's still in the future, but I'm open to it. Meanwhile, I just try to be helpful and kind to troubled people wherever I meet them. That's something I can do right now—it's something we all can do.

Sometimes, when I think people will accept it, I tell them about the day when I saw Jesus and He saved my life. And their eyes light up with hope. They know that even if they can't see Him, if He reached down and helped Bob Bowden out of a tight spot, then He'll surely help them too. And I'm reminded of the words of Jesus Himself: ". . . because thou hast seen me, thou hast believed: blessed are they that have not seen, and yet have believed" (John 20:29 KJV).

THE UNSEEN VISITOR

by Lori White

B e careful!" I called over my shoulder from the bedroom as my two
sons, Jordan, five, and Hunter, three, made a beeline outside to play
in the yard.

It was Friday afternoon and we were moving that weekend from
Conover, North Carolina, down the road a ways to Hickory. My husband
Chan had just pulled into the driveway towing a rugged metal trailer that
he had brought home from our family car dealership to haul some boxes
and small pieces of furniture.

The house and yard were in complete disarray and the boys were having
a blast poking around everything. But just as my friend Joyce and I started
cleaning out the closet, a sickening thud reverberated through the house.

"What in the world—" I started to say to Joyce. An instant later I
heard Chan shout in a voice pinched with panic, "Lori! Lori! Come quick!"

I ran downstairs to the front hall. There I saw Chan, ashen-faced, holding a limp, unrecognizable figure of a little boy covered in blood. Blood
streamed from his mouth, his ears, and from a terrible gash in his head.

"The—the trailer ramp," Chan stammered. "It slammed down on
him when I wasn't looking . . . "

"Dear God . . ." The boy wore green tennis shoes. It was Jordan.

"Lori, we've got to get him to a doctor."

I snatched a blanket off the sofa and we wrapped it around his unconscious form. Joyce stayed behind to watch Hunter as Chan and I leapt into our car. I gunned the engine and the car roared out of the driveway. Chan grabbed the cellular phone and called 911 to have them alert our local hospital that we were coming. As we sped down the road we exchanged frantic glances and tried to soothe Jordan. Chan told him over and over again how much we loved him.

At the emergency room attendants scooped Jordan from Chan's arms. We watched helplessly while medical personnel worked over our boy. Just minutes before, he had been an exuberant child. Chan wrapped his arms around me and I buried my face in his shoulder. A doctor glanced over at us. "We need to transfer him to Frye," he snapped. "They're better equipped." Equipped for what? I wondered, my whole being churning with fear.

Chan and I waited in the treatment room with Jordan and a nurse for the ambulance to Frye Regional Medical Center across town. As Chan signed some documents I stood over Jordan and told him that no matter what happened, his daddy and I loved him and that we were praying.

Suddenly Jordan moved. At first I thought it was my imagination, but Chan and the nurse saw it too. Then, slowly, almost eerily, Jordan raised up to nearly a sitting position, as if someone were gently supporting him with an arm behind his back. His soot-black lashes fluttered open and in a weak but clear voice he said, "Jesus take care of me . . ." His eyes closed peacefully and he sank back down, motionless once again. The nurse looked at us in bewildered disbelief.

Chan half stood, and a cry gathered in my throat. We had taken our boys to church and taught them to pray, but usually they said their prayers at the table and bedtime. Here was Jordan reaching out in a moment of terrible, desperate need. I too would have to reach out with such sure faith. Just then the curtains swept back and Jordan, Chan and I were rushed to a waiting ambulance.

The evening dissolved in a blur. At Frye, Jordan was wheeled straight in for a CAT scan of his brain. Chan's parents, Steve and Jane White were at our side, as were mine, Keith and Paula Turner. Other family and friends had gotten word and come. A minister, Rev. John Misenheimer, and people from church gathered in the emergency room. We were surrounded by folks who loved us and prayed with us. Yet Chan and I didn't know whether our little boy would live.

Finally, Dr. Gregory Rosenfeld, a neurosurgeon, spoke with us. X-rays revealed that Jordan's skull had been fractured by the heavy trailer gate, crushing fragments of bone into the area of the brain that governs speech, hearing and memory. "There is no telling the extent of the damage," Dr. Rosenfeld explained, "until we go in and look." It was only fair, he said, to warn us that the injury was very serious. As Jordan was sped into surgery I broke down and sobbed.

The people who had gathered held hands in prayer. We prayed that the surgeons' skilled hands would be blessed and guided. The love of our friends and family flowed through Chan and me, and an incredible, almost spontaneous feeling of peace and acceptance overpowered our fears. Six hours later Dr. Rosenfeld emerged and, pulling down his surgical mask, motioned us down the hall to a room and opened the door. "Come say hello to Jordan."

Chan and I moved to Jordan's bedside. He was pale and his head was swathed in a turban of bandages. I reached out to him. Oh, Jordan . . . It was then I heard the sweetest sound of my life: A tiny burp erupted from my son, followed by a whispered, "Excuse me."

Not only could Jordan speak, but he still had his manners! By the time they sent him up to the Neuro Intensive Care Unit, he was asking the nurse for a toothbrush. "The doctors don't know what to think about this boy," she said. Still, we were warned that Jordan could take a turn for the worse at any time, and that seizures were a serious possibility with such an invasive head trauma.

Most worrisome, though, was the fear that his brain might develop an infection. Ahead of Jordan lay a series of intravenous antibiotic treatments to fight this potentially fatal complication. We were cautioned that the sessions would be painful for Jordan.

I stayed at Jordan's side all night but could not sleep. Once, near morning, Jordan moaned with nausea and everyone came rushing. I held him and he said, "Mommy, pray with me." Over those next few days, any time he was frightened or suffering, he said, "Mommy, Daddy, come pray with me." That was the beginning of a spiritual journey, with Jordan as my guide. The stronger his faith was, the stronger mine became.

Eventually Jordan was moved from the ICU to the pediatric wing, where the staff was eager to finally meet this "miracle boy." Shortly after his arrival a new therapist pulled me aside. "Mrs. White," the young woman said, "we need to plan your son's treatment. There's a lot of work to be done." Confused, I said, "I don't understand."

She checked her chart. "Isn't your boy the one with the depressed skull fracture?"

"Yes, but he just got up and walked to the bathroom. He's been talking nonstop all day and he's building a house with his Legos."

"That's incredible," the therapist replied and went to see for herself.

The technician who had done Jordan's initial CAT scan also stopped by. "I felt so sorry for you that night," she told Chan and me. "I never thought you'd get your boy back this well or this quickly. I wasn't sure you'd get him back at all. I've never seen anything like it."

In fact, the only thing keeping Jordan in the hospital was the intravenous antibiotic treatments—a harrowing twice-daily ordeal that took thirty minutes for the burning, powerful medicine to be completely transfused into Jordan's body. Every time Jordan wailed out in pain he begged, "Pray for me, Mommy. Pray." And I would, as hard as I knew how. Poor Chan. After a while he couldn't stand to be in the room.

The ordeal exhausted me too. One night before the next treatment, while Jordan was sleeping, I felt as if I couldn't possibly endure another minute. Yet I knew he was counting on me. Kneeling by Jordan's bed I buried my face in his blanket. "Lord," I quietly pleaded, "all I can do is trust You the way Jordan trusts You. Please protect Jordan from the pain."

The door opened quietly behind me as I got up and lay down on the bed beside Jordan. I wrapped my arms around him. When the nurse shifted his arm to put in the IV he started to move. I patted him and whispered, "It's okay. Mommy's here. Mommy's praying." He closed his eyes again.

Nurses stood by ready to help when the burning and crying started. The room was still and dark and hushed. Drip by drip the medicine entered Jordan's vein. Ten minutes. Twenty. Thirty minutes passed and it was over. Not once did my little boy stir.

The doctors were able to release Jordan after only ten days in the hospital. There was no sign of infection, and we brought him home to complete his recovery. He is continuing to heal, with only some loss of hearing in his right ear.

For a time Jordan didn't remember anything about the accident, but then one day while he was playing with a toy truck he suddenly said, "Mommy, I pulled the pin out. That's what made the trailer ramp fall on me." I stopped what I was doing. "It really hurt," he went on, "but then Jesus came."

I tried to sound calm. "What did Jesus look like, honey?"

"He was just . . . all white. Then Daddy came and lifted the ramp off my head." The gate had weighed nearly three hundred pounds and Chan had said many times that he was amazed he had been able to raise it so easily.

"Jesus came to see me when we got to the hospital too," Jordan continued. His delicate features were set in an expression of deep, unperturbed seriousness. A feeling tingled up my back. "He lifted me up and hugged me and said, 'Jordan, you're going to be okay now.'"

My mind flew back to that moment in the treatment room waiting for the ambulance to Frye when Jordan mysteriously rose up in bed, as if cradled by an unseen visitor, and spoke. Had he really seen someone at that instant, someone only a hurt little child could see? I knelt and wrapped my arms around Jordan, and as I did I could sense another set of arms enfolding us both, arms that are always close when we are in need.

Come, my Way, my Truth, my Life:
such a way as gives us breath;
such a truth as ends all strife;
such a life as killeth death.

—GEORGE HERBERT

THE REFUGEE GUESTS

by Bill Fero

When our church put out a call in 1977 seeking housing for a Vietnamese refugee family, I wanted no part of it. Then my aunt came to me.

"No one else seems to have room for them," she pleaded. "They just need a place to stay until they can get settled and start new lives." She touched my arm. "You live alone in this big farmhouse with all these bedrooms."

"No," I growled, shaking my head. The last thing I wanted around me was anyone from Vietnam. Then I hesitated; a diabolical thought had crossed my mind.

"On second thought, Aunt Rose," I said, "why not?"

After she happily hurried out to her car I gripped the arms of my wheelchair, overwhelmed by flashbacks. In my mind a brilliant explosion blinded me as a booby trap blew up under my feet. Again I found myself awakening in a hospital to discover my legs were gone. I had been a naive nineteen-year-old when I enlisted in the army in 1968 and volunteered for Vietnam. The horror of jungle fighting, of seeing buddies blown to bits, of three agonizing years in Army hospitals had turned me into a zombie by the time I reentered civilian life.

I tried to forget my pain through alcohol and drugs. I believed God didn't exist. Concerned family members convinced me to buy a small farm near my hometown, Whitewater, and I got a machinist's job at the nearby General Motors plant. During off-hours I gardened, and kept some horses, pigs and chickens.

But my bitterness and self-pity festered. Most of my friends were Vietnam vets, and as we traded war stories at bars, my smoldering resentment flared into a burning hatred for all Vietnamese.

So as Aunt Rose drove to the minister's house that day, I sat relishing my fiendish scheme. I would make the Vietnamese family my servants. I would make them pay for the agony I had suffered.

In my ancient hand-controlled GMC camper truck, I picked up the family at the Rock County Airport a week later. They huddled in the terminal, Papa San Phi, Mama San, three young boys and a girl. As I rolled up they stared at me in surprise, not prepared for my condition. But they quickly recovered, giving me hesitant smiles; overly polite, we exchanged greetings in their limited English and my pidgin Vietnamese. As I drove them to the farm they were quiet.

I showed them around the house and outbuildings. Though I pointed out several bedrooms, they seemed spooked by the big old house and wanted to sleep together in one room.

The next morning I put my plan into action. I barked out orders. "Papa San, you weed garden." "Mama San, clean kitchen, scrub floor."

I pointed to the youngsters, "You go feed the pigs and chickens." All of them smiled and hurried off. Mama San began filling a scrub bucket.

As they labored I briskly wheeled among them like a drill sergeant. "Don't spill that corn." "Careful with the hoe." "Get the mop under the stove, Mama San." They worked with alacrity. When they finished, I ordered Mama San to cook dinner.

That evening they went off to bed after wishing me good night. I sat in my wheelchair feeling cheated. Instead of cowering in humiliation or seething in resentment, they had responded cheerfully, even seemed eager to help and please me. *Oh well,* I figured, *wait till they've been here a bit. They'll find out.*

But the next few days saw no dampening of their enthusiasm. Despite my ranting and cursing, they finished their tasks with smiles and polite bows. Their attitude was getting my goat. But nothing prepared me for what happened after I took Mama San and her daughter to the barn. Pointing to a stall, I made shoveling motions and barked, "Muck it out good."

One boy pushed me back toward the house, where I got Papa San started on painting a shed. As the day wore on the mother and daughter seemed to be taking longer than necessary, so I had one of the youngsters wheel me to the barn. As I reached it the two emerged laughing and talking, slacks smeared with manure and dirt, strands of black hair plastered to their foreheads. I figured they had been goofing off instead of working.

I rolled into the barn to inspect their work and froze in surprise. The two had mucked out all seven stalls, and cleaned the ceilings! What was their game?

Rankled, I charged into the house, grabbed my bowling ball and drove into town. I came home at 2:00 AM and banged on the family's bedroom door. "Mama San," I roared, "get up! Fix me something to eat!" Soon she appeared bowing and smiling.

I hunched grimly in my chair as she went to work at the stove. She set a steaming noodle dish before me. My first impulse was to taste it, push it away and berate her. But it was delicious and I finished it in silence.

That night I fell asleep wondering when these people would break. Next morning I told the family to wash the dirt-encrusted windows of the chicken coop. (I believe the old shed hadn't been cleaned since the farm was built.)

After a few hours I wheeled out to the coop. I stuck my head through the door and caught my breath. Not only were the windows spotless but so were the walls and ceiling.

I pushed back into the house muttering. They were trying to make a fool of me! Within several months I had the cleanest farm in Walworth County. The children picked up English quickly and through them the family learned how I lost my legs; they expressed nothing but sympathy.

Then one day Papa San apologetically announced, "We have family now in California; they ask us to come help in their store."

So off they went. *That's all right,* I thought. *I'll find some other servants who won't be so willing to please.* Another Vietnamese family soon moved in. They too labored under my despotism. And they too responded in the same smiling manner.

By then I had tired of yelling and cursing, as it seemed not to bother my guests. But I was still tough with work assignments. After some months the second family left for permanent locations and in came Chau, his wife and two children. Chau spoke fairly good English and one evening when we were talking after supper it became obvious he was reluctantly trying to tell me something.

Finally, I wormed it out of him.

"It . . . it's what the other families say about you," he said.

I steeled myself. Whatever it was, I knew I had it coming.

He continued, "They . . . say how nice you are." He blinked and coughed apologetically. "But you just have little problem with your voice . . . and angry all the time. They don't know why you don't enjoy life."

Chau cringed as if he expected me to strike him. But I could only stare down at my stumps, hot shame rising in me. I had tried so hard to hate these people, but it wasn't working anymore. I was beginning to like them. Their kindness was wearing me down.

As if that weren't enough, somehow they had found out when my birthday was. For a long time I had not paid the day any attention; what was there to celebrate? But on a March day in 1979 a load of cards and packages arrived in the mail. Colorful hand-drawn greetings and carefully scripted messages read, "To good man, Mr. Bill . . . We never forget you . . . Thank you for helping us in new land."

I broke down crying. The gentle people I had so spitefully used were repaying me with love and understanding. In my anger I had turned away from the Lord, but these people, some Buddhist, some Christian, had exemplified a Christlike spirit. They had done what Jesus urged his followers to do: "Bless them that curse you, do good to them that hate you, and pray for them which despitefully use you, and persecute you" (Matthew 5:44 KJV).

At that moment something happened to me. A warmth began to melt the icy shell I had built around me, and for the first time since I had lost my legs I felt like living again. I couldn't hate anymore. I could only ask for forgiveness.

Since then more than forty Vietnamese refugees have stayed with me on their way to beginning new lives in America. Moreover, our relationship has given me a calling. Concerned about the grinding poverty and lack of medical supplies in Vietnam, I started making the rounds of hospitals and medical-supply companies for pharmaceuticals and surgical equipment that I then shipped there.

I have accompanied the shipments many times, returning to the country I had once blamed so bitterly for taking my legs. Now, thanks to its loving emissaries, I have been given a new life. I took refugees into my house, but they are the ones who made it a home.

IN HIS ARMS

by Florence Van Horn

I was facing another long night in the intensive care unit, where I was a nurse. The ICU can be one of the toughest assignments in a hospital, and I was also on call for emergency room duty. I was exhausted; my joints throbbed with pain and my legs ached. *If I can only make it through this shift,* I thought.

A large ring of keys jangled in my pocket as I headed to the medication room. With each step, I was more aware of the jangling—because I knew those keys offered a solution.

Not a soul was in sight as I opened the double-locked narcotics cabinet and prepared Mr. Johnson's intravenous morphine. Sitting on one of the shelves was a package of Percodan, a potent pain medication. I tried not to look at it, but my eyes kept roving back. As I finished up with Mr. Johnson's medicine, my hand snaked out for the Percodan. *I'll only take one this time,* I promised myself.

A surge of relief flowed through me as I peeled back the wrapper covering the round yellow pill. I filled a paper cup with water to wash it down. Then I quickly locked up and headed for Mr. Johnson's room.

Just a year earlier, in May of 1979, I had graduated from nursing school. I'd become a nurse at age twenty-nine because I wanted to help people, and because I needed a good-paying job; after my marriage broke up I was left with two children to support. But nursing was more than a job; it was a way for me to find an identity and a sense of self-worth, things that I had searched for all my life. Now, however, I was letting it all slip away and I hated myself for it.

Soon it became nearly impossible for me to make it through a shift without taking some narcotics. And the drugs I used were stronger and stronger. In the bustle of the hospital, no one seemed to wonder about my frequent trips to the bathroom or my willingness to help other nurses dispense medicines. I rarely missed work, because that was where the drugs were, and I tried to be "super nurse" to avert suspicion.

I was an addict. I made excuses and vowed to quit. I was tired, or I wasn't feeling well, or I was working a double shift. This is just to help you work, to ease the pain. But I knew I had a deeper, lurking pain that I was avoiding.

I changed jobs frequently, always keeping a half-step ahead of discovery. I was getting more reckless all the time, and self-loathing was eating me alive. I remember one day a patient complimented me. "Miss Van Horn," he said as I took his pulse, "you're the best nurse I've run into around here." I tried to keep up a smile, but I could feel myself collapsing inside.

I had just signed out a morphine dose in his name.

One spring morning in 1985, when I was working in a state psychiatric hospital, a young woman slashed her wrist with the flip top of a soda can. It was a clumsy, desperate attempt at suicide. As I cleaned her wound and tried to comfort her, she looked up at me. "You don't know what it's like to be abused by your parents," she snarled. "I don't believe in God and I don't trust anybody. Just stay away from me."

Her words stung like a slap in the face. And there in that room the distance between myself and my patient vanished. I was as sick as this poor young woman, perhaps sicker. At least she could say aloud what I tried to smother with drugs.

While my coworkers ate lunch, I slipped an entire pack of Demerol into my pocket. I locked myself in a bathroom stall and loaded the syringe four times, begging the drug for relief. At home that night, while my teenage sons were watching television, I closed the door to my bedroom and injected the rest of the Demerol. It was enough to kill me, and I didn't care. I simply did not want to feel any more pain. I was a disgrace to my profession, a liar and a thief, and a poor mother to my sons. They'll be better off without me.

I slept for twenty-two straight hours, a deep, numbing sleep. My sons, who were used to me working and sleeping long hours, didn't disturb me, though they were concerned. They had pretty much figured out what my problem was. At work too people were beginning to suspect. Soon it would be time to change jobs again.

As I lay on the bed, too tired and broken even to pray, the words of the desperate young woman in the hospital the day before came back: *You don't know what it's like to be abused by your parents.*

But I did know. From the age of five I had been abused. Now the memories rushed over me.

From outside, the big, white two-story house I grew up in looked safe and happy, just the kind of house a high-standing, churchgoing family like ours was supposed to live in. But inside I had lived a life of terror. My father was abusive in every way, and intimidating, and my mother was addicted to tranquilizers. After school I would try to sneak into the house without my mother noticing, and creep to my hiding place in the attic. I'd hide there for as long as I could, praying to Jesus that my father not find me. But eventually I'd have to come out. My only relief was Sunday school, where I learned about Jesus.

Each year of my childhood, I slipped deeper and deeper into my shell. Once I overheard a teacher discussing me: "She's such a quiet child. Her eyes. They almost look as if no one lives behind them." But what lived behind them was a terrorized, guilt-ridden little girl who felt that she was responsible for all the bad things that kept happening to her.

I didn't trust anyone enough to tell them. And no one would believe such a thing about my parents. But one night when I was thirteen, I made a desperate decision. I looked my father right in the eye and said, "If you ever lay a finger on me again, I swear I will commit suicide." From that day on he left me alone. As soon as I turned seventeen, I married and moved away.

Curled on the bed after my Demerol stupor, I awoke to a stark realization: More than twenty years after that horrible promise to my father, I was still trying to act on it. I was slowly killing myself with drugs. I stepped unsteadily into the bathroom and stared in the mirror—haggard, bleary eyed, ashen. I was doing the same thing to myself that my patient in the hospital had tried. I closed my eyes and wept.

Through bitter tears one last childhood memory returned. It was from my Sunday school classroom, the only place where I had felt safe as a girl. There was a picture hanging on the wall. I could stare at it for hours and feel peaceful. It was of Jesus cradling a little lamb tenderly in His arms. My teacher had explained that Jesus cared most for the lost lamb and rejoiced at its return. When I imagined Jesus holding me I felt loved, cared for and protected.

Standing before the mirror, I had never felt more lost in my life—I couldn't imagine ever being found again, not even by Jesus. But I knew I could not live any longer without Him, and I cried out, "Jesus, please find me. Please help me. I am so lost." Then I pictured myself being held in His arms like the lost lamb of my childhood.

The following day I walked into the Director of Nursing's office, closed the door and told her the truth. She helped me find a drug treatment center that stressed spiritual principles. Slowly, during the weeks I was there, I began to realize that to recover from my addiction I had to face my childhood. And to recover from my childhood, I had to face my addiction. I could do neither without entrusting my entire being—nurse, drug addict, mother, abused child—to the care of the loving Shepherd.

I have been free of chemical dependency for nine years now. Today I am a nurse for the reason I became one—to help people. I have been involved with support groups for medical professionals with drug and alcohol problems. I've tried to make amends for all that I can. But most of all, my recovery continues to be a spiritual recovery. It is the road on which I am never lost.

Like as Christ was raised up from the dead by the glory of the Father, even so we also should walk in newness of life.

—ROMANS 6:4 (KJV)

THE PROMISE I NEEDED

by Sandra Simpson LeSourd

As a child, I loved Jesus. But as an adult, I let Him down, lost in a self-destructive lifestyle of alcohol and prescription drugs. Good Friday in those years plunged me into an abyss of suicidal depression. Reconciliation with God, my sins forgiven, the promise of new life—all seemed so unattainable. Even after I recovered sobriety, I spent much of Good Friday weeping, identifying with Jesus and His agony on the cross.

Then came the Good Friday when something changed inside me. Life was beginning to make sense again, but I still needed hope and direction for the future. I was reading the account of the crucifixion, weeping as always. Suddenly I was struck by the conversation between the two thieves who were crucified with Jesus, and Jesus' response. Where one criminal cursed Jesus, the other admitted his wrongdoing and said, "'This Man has done nothing wrong.' Then he said to Jesus, 'Lord, remember me when You come into Your kingdom.' And Jesus said to him, 'Assuredly, I say to you, today you will be with Me in Paradise'" (Luke 23:41–43 NKJV).

Chills raced through my body as I read those words. This was the promise I needed. Like the sinful thief, I was now honest, penitent, a seeker. I too had poured out my heart to Jesus.

And He was there with me now. "Sandy you, too, will be with Me in paradise."

THE CHOICE

by Ruth Vaughn

My brother Joe stood beside my open coffin, granite-faced in sorrow. His wife Frances sat on a fallen log nearby, her hunched shoulders shaking. Lying in my casket in Morgan Mill Cemetery, where generations of my family lay buried, I looked up at Joe and Frances, grateful to know they cared so much. They would miss me, I knew, but they would be all right.

My choice was clear: life or death. And I knew what I wanted. Deliberately I reached up to pull the casket lid down. After all the suffering, all the sorrow, I would be free of pain at last.

But as the opening narrowed to just inches, I stopped. I gasped. *What on earth have I been thinking? My sons. They still need me!*

I threw open the lid, sat up and found myself staring directly into the face of my doctor. "You've been in a coma for three days," he said, telling me I'd had a toxic reaction to my sleep medication.

I looked around, trying to get my bearings. Though my vision was blurry, out of focus, I could identify the narrow hospital bed, the IV dripping. "Toxic reaction to this drug," my doctor explained, "can include visual disruptions, coma, and for some, death."

I dared not speak. I hardly trusted myself to move. For the reality my doctor was describing was so totally different from the equally vivid world

I had just left behind, a world where I had fought and won battles, a world where I had only moments ago chosen life over death.

A nurse came in to consult with the doctor about another patient. I noticed a poinsettia on my dressing table, a tiny Christmas tree, a couple of festively wrapped gifts. Oh yes. It was December.

After the nurse left, the doctor studied my chart. "Everything's under control," he said. "You've survived and your vision should be normal within a few days. But prepare yourself for tonight. You probably won't sleep. Your system has to cleanse out the toxicity, and because of the drug, I can't give you any sleep medication."

As my eyes followed him out the door, I found myself half-expecting the door to open again to admit a blond, blue-eyed, smiling man, the man who had been my rock and my comfort during each of my many hospital stays during our thirty years of marriage. Part of me knew, knew for certain, that he would not come. Yet my heart didn't believe that at all.

It all still seemed so impossible. I always knew I might get cancer. That was a possibility. I always knew I might fall into an earthquake crack. That was a possibility. Even Addison's disease, which had robbed my body of hormones since 1976, sapped me of my strength and reduced me to skin and bones. That was a possibility. But there was one thing that I'd thought would never happen to me: divorce. That was not how I loved. My marriage was too sacred, divorce unthinkable.

Nonetheless, he was gone.

I was alone.

For the first time in my life, in December 1987, I was having to face a hospital crisis without a loving husband present.

Night brought for other patients merciful sleep, but not for me. As the night wore on, my body became more and more agitated till eventually my arms were flopping around, hopelessly out of control.

But far greater than the physical distress was the emotional anguish.

The one person who had vowed to honor and cherish me in sickness and in health had proved faithless. Throughout this long night, except for the nurse who periodically checked on me, the flickering light of the television would be my only companion. *He's gone, Ruth,* the motionless door seemed to shout every time I glanced at it. *Gone, and never coming back.*

Ever since the divorce I had felt like one of those spiral shells washed up on a beach. Poke a toothpick in and around, you find nothing there. Was a life like that worth living?

Only hours before, in another reality, God had offered me a choice. Had I lowered my casket lid only a few inches more, my suffering would have been all over by now. I felt sure of it. Now I was wondering, had I made the wrong choice?

In my coma world I had fought for my boys and won. I had been in a boxing ring, arms coiled, fists clenched. From the sidelines I had heard Ronnie and Billy cheering me on. "You'll win, Mom. You'll win for us." And I knew I would. I always had. That's what a mother does.

It was for my boys that I had chosen life. But through that tormented night I wondered: *Even if I am alive for my boys, in my condition—sick, confined, dependent—what use will I be to them?*

Why, God? I cried silently into the darkness. *Why won't You work a miracle to make the world all right again?* I must have asked Him a hundred questions.

And God was silent.

I was totally alone.

Hour after sleepless hour, I hurled accusations and demanded explanations. Yet as much as I wanted God to explain, there was something I wanted more, much more. I needed to know there was a God who knew my name, who knew my need, who knew me. A God who cared for me, one small woman in Presbyterian Hospital in Oklahoma City.

When at long last pastel streaks began erasing the night's blackness, my despair only deepened. I didn't want another day to come! My lifelong belief in a loving God was teetering. This notion of omnipotence caring for one fragile, frail human heart—was it all only wishful thinking? During that long night I had found no reassurance that my faith was rooted in fact.

During that next day, and the next, and the next, I saw no such evidence. If God really cared, why didn't He show me?

Then came the morning when the doctor decided I should put my legs to the test. Trembling, they held me upright and, haltingly, shakily, moved me forward. The doctor grinned and invited me to take a walk in the hall.

I pulled my blue chenille robe on over my hospital gown, stepped into slippers, and eased out the door. After my days in a coma world filled with events as vivid as any I have ever known, I had begun to wonder: Had I been hallucinating? I had feared I might be in the psychiatric ward. Now I read with relief the sign on the door: RUTH VAUGHN—ENDOCRINOLOGY—.

I walked the empty corridor on unsteady legs. From a closed room I could hear a voice. "Sweet little Jesus boy. . ." it sang, but I hardly noticed, and kept on moving. Then suddenly a phrase in the song stopped me cold: "We didn't know who You was."

It was only a husky voice on television, only a Christmas carol in December, but inside an empty shell, a new life began to stir.

Oh, God, I see it now. I wasn't hallucinating. You were there in that boxing ring, giving me the strength to fight. In the coffin too, You were there, giving me the choice of living or dying—then reminding me of my two boys who needed me.

But as the lyric floated through the door, enfolding me, I realized that the same God who had allowed me to choose to live or die had also compressed Himself into human flesh, to suffer and die, so I would know that in my suffering I am never alone.

As I walked on down the hall, the words of the spiritual followed me: "But please, Sir, forgive us, Lord . . . We didn't know 'twas You."

· PART 7 ·

Glimpses of Jesus as Our Peace

IN JOHN 14:27 (NIV) JESUS TELLS HIS DISCIPLES: "Peace I leave with you; my peace I give you." That's a strong statement, but the apostle Paul is even more direct, saying that Jesus "himself is our peace" (Ephesians 2:14 NIV).

The stories in this section show how various writers have found Christ's comforting, peacegiving presence—sometimes in the midst of trauma, sometimes in life's ordinary tasks and days. Several of these stories involve parent-child relationships. This isn't surprising, as often our deepest worries are not so much for ourselves as for those we love.

Catherine Marshall and Kathie Kania provide insights about prayer that have helped me better appreciate God's love and mercy and also appropriate a powerful scriptural blessing: "May the Lord of peace himself give you peace at all times and in every way" (2 Thessalonians 3:16 NIV). May you claim that inner peace for yourself and your loved ones today.

THE WOMAN FROM NOWHERE

by Laura Z. Sowers

My preschooler son Marc and I were shopping in a large department store. On our way down to the main floor, Marc hopped on the escalator. I followed. Suddenly Marc screamed. I'd never heard a sound like that before. "Mama! My foot!"

Marc's right foot was wedged between the side of the moving step and the escalator's wall. His body was twisted toward me. He screamed again. The escalator continued downward.

In the panic of the moment, the danger at the bottom of the escalator flashed before me, the thought of the foot being severed—

"Turn off the escalator!" I screamed. "Somebody help!" And then, "Oh, dear God, dear God, help us! Help us!"

Several people at the base of the escalator began a flurry of activity. The escalator stopped! Someone had pressed an emergency button at the bottom of the steps.

Thank You, Father, I prayed.

Marc clutched my arm and cried while I struggled to get a better look at his foot. A chill raced up my spine when I saw the tiny space in which his foot was trapped. It looked no more than a quarter of an inch wide. All I could see of his foot was his heel. The rest had disappeared into the jaws of the machine.

"Someone call the fire department!" I shouted.

Marc looked up at me desperately. "Mama," he said, "pray!"

I crouched next to him, holding him. I prayed. For a moment he quieted. Soon, though, he began crying again. "Daddy! Daddy!" he called out. I shouted out our business phone number, hoping someone would call my husband.

The two of us sat waiting. Marc cried. I patted his head. As the minutes passed I could see dark images of crutches and wheelchairs. I had always taken for granted that our little son would grow up playing baseball and soccer, running on strong legs and sturdy feet. Now, nothing seemed certain.

My prayers were as scattered as my feelings, and I searched my memory for a Bible verse to hold on to.

"And we know that all things work together for good to them that love God, to them who are the called according to His purpose" (Romans 8:28 KJV). This was one of the few verses I had memorized.

"You promised, Lord!" I cried. "And we know that all things . . ." Over and over I said that verse. ". . . called according to His purpose."

Marc looked up at me and said, "Mama, my bones feel broken and bleedy."

I clutched his blond head tighter to me, but now it was I who was feeling faint. *I can't faint, Lord,* I prayed. *Marc needs me—oh, Lord, I know You're here! Where? Help me!*

At that moment I felt warm soft arms enfolding me from behind. A woman's soothing voice said quietly in my ear, "Jesus is here, Jesus is here."

The woman had come down the escalator and sat on the step above me. She gently rocked me from side to side, surrounding my shaking body with a calm embrace. "Tell your son his foot is all right," she said in my ear. There was an assurance in her voice.

"Marc," I said into his ear. "Your foot is all right."

"Tell him you'll buy him a new pair of shoes—whatever kind he wants."

"I'll buy you a new pair of shoes. Any kind you like."

Marc's crying stopped. "Cowboy boots? Like Daddy's?" We were talking about new shoes—new shoes for two healthy feet! For the first time since the ordeal began, I felt hope. Maybe, just maybe, his foot really would be all right.

"Tell him there are no broken bones," she said.

I did.

The firemen arrived. Two men with crowbars pried the step away from the escalator wall, freeing Marc's foot at last. His shoe was in tatters, it took all my courage to watch as the men pulled the shredded sock off Marc's foot, but when they did, they revealed a red, bruised, but whole foot.

I turned to share my joy with my wonderful friend, but all I saw was her leg as she rounded the corner at the top of the escalator. I never even saw her face.

My husband Craig arrived just as the firemen were setting Marc down on the floor. He was still sobbing, but he could wiggle his toes. Later, X-rays confirmed what I already knew: no broken bones, only bruises and swelling.

To this day I do not know who the woman was who helped me, who knew that Jesus was there with us, who knew that the Lord keeps His promises.

Many people have suggested that the woman was an angel of the Lord. I can't be sure about that, but of this I am certain: She was heaven-sent.

TAKE A WALK WITH JESUS

by Marilyn Morgan King

The afternoon before my daughter's school play, Karen was suddenly seized by an attack of stage fright. I thought of suggesting that she study her lines some more, but I changed my mind. We went for a silent walk instead. We agreed not to talk, but we stopped to pet a dog, picked up a few unusually pretty stones on a graveled road, smelled some lilacs and watched the sky turn from a bright glare to a soft, restful pumpkin color. When we got home, Karen was relaxed. The stage fright was gone, the play went well and she had discovered a very effective tranquilizer—one that can't be purchased in any pharmacy.

If you're feeling nervous about something today, put on your coat, tell your family or coworkers you'll be back in a few minutes and take a walk with Jesus. As you walk, meditate on His words, "Peace I leave with you, My peace I give unto you" (John 14:27 KJV). Silently repeat the words over and over as you walk, letting their truth flow gently through you. Try it. You'll be surprised at how self-composed you'll feel when you get back to your daily tasks.

THE GIRL NOBODY WANTED

by Stephanie Fast

After the end of the Korean war I was conceived by the union of a Korean woman with an American soldier, probably in the city of Pusan. As a child of mixed blood, I was considered a nonperson. I was abandoned at about the age of four and began living on the streets. Many orphaned children of mixed blood were killed; others were picked off the streets and sent to America by adoption agencies. I wasn't.

I learned to snatch morsels from food stalls, to be at butcher shops when they threw out the bones, and to roast grasshoppers on rice straw. At night I'd roll myself into a straw mat and sleep under a bridge. I never dreamed of acceptance from adults; I was a half-breed—a dirty "toogee"—an ugly reminder of an ugly war. Even other street children taunted me. They'd send me to steal food, reasoning that as a nonperson I wouldn't feel the pain of a beating if I got caught.

Once I was tied to a waterwheel and nearly drowned. Another time I was thrown down an abandoned well. I screamed for help until I had no more voice, then watched as the patch of light at the top turned to darkness. I found a stone sticking out of the wall and sat there, cold and numb. I wondered how long it would be before I was dead. Then I heard the voice of an old woman: "Little girl, are you down there?"

After she hauled me out with the well's bucket, she hurried me to a barn and covered me with straw. Kind as she was, she didn't want to be seen helping a *toogee*, for fear of what her neighbors would do to her. That's why she had waited till dark to help me. "You sleep now, little girl, but before daylight, run to the mountains. If they find you here tomorrow, they'll kill you."

At dawn I fled to a mountain cave and hid. That night, huddled alone, I peered out at the stars. *Why am I so bad*, I wondered, *that people want to kill me? Why can't I be like other children, who have a mommy and daddy?*

I began going from village to village, thinking, *Maybe my mom lives in one of them and will recognize me.*

One day I went to the train station and stood on the platform, waiting until a train pulled in. People began spewing out of the cars, and forgetting all caution, I scurried among them, craning my neck and peering into the women's eyes so the one who was my mother could recognize me.

Any moment now, my mind raced, a woman's face will light up and she'll say, "My little girl! At last I have found you!"

But no one stopped. Time after time women brushed me out of their paths. Instead of lighting up, their eyes narrowed. I knew what they were thinking. *Toogee.* The platform emptied. Just a few American soldiers stood about. Maybe one of them is my daddy. I went to them. But none of the soldiers even saw the American in me. To them I was just like all the other little beggars who filled the streets of Pusan. One of them gave me a chocolate bar that I wolfed down.

I was about seven when a cholera epidemic swept Korea. One day I fainted in the street. When I woke up I was on a mat in a bright room filled with children. A Swedish nurse had brought me to the World Vision orphanage in Taejon. I recovered and was soon strong enough to wash diapers and help feed and care for the babies.

One day the nurse told me that an American couple was coming to adopt a baby boy. I took extra care with my boys to make them look appealing. We were out in a courtyard when they arrived—huge people with pale faces like moons. The man came over, picked up one of my boys and lovingly stroked the baby's face. Then I watched in disbelief as tears welled in the man's eyes.

I inched closer to get a better look at this strange man. He placed the baby gently back in his basket, turned to me and then began to caress my face. My heart thumped wildly; his touch felt so good. But I had never, ever been touched except to be beaten or kicked. Child of the streets that I was, I slapped his hand away, spit at him and ran.

The next day this man and his wife returned. They talked to the nurse and pointed at me. Even though I was nearly nine, I weighed only thirty pounds. I had worms, my body was covered with scars, my hair crawled with lice. I had a lazy eye that flopped around in its socket. But David and Judy Merwin chose me.

When I entered their house, I thought I'd come to a palace. I was overwhelmed by their kindness and love. Patiently, painstakingly, they taught me English and helped me with my lessons at the American school. After a while they took me back to America, provided the best home life, the best education; they gave me their all. I was living in a fairyland, and yet I was not a part of it. Deep down I still felt like a *toogee*.

I learned early that Americans like it when you smile, so I did a lot of smiling. As a young teen in Rockport, Indiana, I made many friends. Everyone loved the pleasant Korean girl who sang in the choir, taught Sunday school and got academic awards. I smiled to please everyone because I never wanted to go back to street life again. But deep down the gnawing fear always lurked: If they only knew who I really was, they would hate me.

My mother and father were disappointed when I insisted on bleaching my hair and buying deep-blue contact lenses so I could look more American. My orange hair looked strange and I lived in a dark-blue world, but I thought it was an improvement.

I put up a pretty good front in public, but at home I became withdrawn and irritable. I had temper tantrums, and I spent a lot of time in my room, brooding under the covers. I hated it, but the *toogee* began to take over my life. When Mom questioned me, I clammed up. Mom and Dad should never, never find out about my life as a street kid. I was convinced that if they did they'd shun me.

One night after Mom confronted me about my sullenness, I ran to my room, so upset that I didn't dare speak to her for fear I'd lash out and ruin everything. I looked in the mirror behind the closed door of my bedroom. "You haven't changed anything," I hissed at myself. "You're still nothing but a dirty *toogee*, a piece of trash."

I ran to my bed and buried myself under the covers, fully clothed. Now you've done it, I thought, cringing. Mom and Dad are probably wishing they'd taken that little boy . . .

My bedroom door opened, and my father called softly, "Stephanie."

I pulled the covers away from my face and looked at him. His face was grave. *Oh no. He's going to tell me they want me to leave . . .*

He sat in a chair by my bed and reached for my hand. "Your mother and I want you to know that we love you very much, but you seem to have a hard time accepting that love. The time has come for us to release you to God. You know the Bible; I don't have to tell you that God loves you . . ."

He fell silent, his jaw working as he groped for words. Finally he said, "Think of Jesus, Stephanie. He has walked in your shoes. He knows exactly how you feel. He's the only one who can help you." My father hugged me and left the room.

For a long time I lay there, turning over in my mind what Dad had said about Jesus. He was born in hard circumstances, straw was His blanket as it had been mine, and He had to flee because, like me, some people wanted to kill Him.

For the first time in years I felt a strange sensation on my cheeks. Tears. Deep inside me something hard and cold had broken—something that had been standing between me and the love of my dear family and God.

I wept for Jesus, who understood about love but had to die for us anyway. I wept for the girl who finally had been loved, but still had chosen to listen to the voices that taunted her. And I wept in relief: Jesus knew all about me and still loved me.

A sprout of self-worth started growing in me that afternoon. As my anger melted away, so did my sullenness and outbursts. I let my hair grow back naturally and threw away the blue contact lenses. And then one day I looked in the mirror, regarded the face smiling at me and said, "God thinks you're beautiful, Stephanie, and so do I."

I WON'T BE HOME
FOR CHRISTMAS

by Pat Brewster

Anne called right as I was unwrapping the figures of my Nativity set. "Anne, I've been thinking about you!" I said. My daughter lived several hundred miles away. After eighteen years of marriage and three children, she'd just been through a divorce. This would be her first Christmas as a single mom.

Thank goodness she and the children would be spending it with our entire family. My son and his wife had invited all of us to their house. Christmas in Connecticut! Just what Anne needed. She and the kids would be surrounded by family, and everything would be all right again.

"How are you doing?" I asked. "I can't wait to see you. . . ."

"Mom, that's why I'm calling. I won't be there for Christmas. The kids and I talked it over. We want to spend the day here at our own place."

She couldn't possibly mean what she was saying.

"Mom? Are you there . . . ?"

"Anne, are you sure?" I tried to keep the disappointment out of my voice.

"I'm sure." Anne's tone was firm. "The kids and I need to stay put this year. I think it's important. You'll have a good time without us."

But what about you? I thought. I hung up and forced myself to finish unwrapping the Nativity figures and arrange them on a shelf. When I tried to set up my red and green candles in a holly centerpiece, I came to a complete stop.

It's not just Christmas, I realized. *How will Anne go on with the rest of her life?* Like every mother, I'd hoped that my children's lives would be fulfilling, peaceful and secure. Now Anne was starting over, on her own, with three children to raise.

I couldn't imagine it. I pushed the tissue wrappings aside and looked out the window. Worry settled around me like frost crystallizing on the glass. *Anne's been through so much. She needs her family. She needs to be with us.*

I phoned my son's wife. "Anne says she's not coming," I said. "I tried to talk her out of it, but she wouldn't listen."

"Well, she knows she's welcome and we'll miss her," my daughter-in-law said. "But if it's what Anne wants, I understand. She's had a tough year."

Exactly. That's why she should be with us this Christmas.

December raced by. Wrapping presents for Anne and her kids was a painful reminder that she would be apart from us. "Maybe Anne will change her mind," I said to John. But she didn't. At the last minute I squeezed their gifts into the car trunk, just in case.

Snowflakes drifted from the sky as my husband and I drove to our son's on Christmas Eve. "Grandma! Grandpa!" There was a rush of kisses and hugs and the stamping of boots.

That night all twenty of us went to early Christmas Eve Mass. The candlelit church was crowded with families. Music filled the air. As the priest read from Luke—"Unto you is born this day in the city of David, a savior"—an infant cried. The priest looked up from the text, pleased. "Right on cue," he murmured.

My heart was lifted by Christmas joy. Yet I also felt sad for Anne and her children. Sad they weren't with the family. Sad that my daughter's hopes and dreams had been shattered. Sad that there was nothing I could do.

The next morning it was a free-for-all. The children tore open gifts and grown-ups exclaimed over new slippers. Stepping through mounds of ribbon and paper, I went into the bedroom and called Anne. "Merry Christmas," I said, trying to sound lighthearted. "How's it going?"

"Mom, the kids and I are having the best day!" She chatted on about the dusting of snow they'd gotten and all the presents. "Some friends just dropped by. We're going ice-skating." My daughter's voice was cheerful. More than cheerful. She sounded strong. Then the grandchildren got on. "Hi, Grandma!"

For the next day or two I put my worries aside and enjoyed the rest of the time with my family. Anne and the girls had sounded okay. *Maybe they will be all right,* I told myself. But when John and I got home and walked into our house, my apprehension returned.

I spent most of the next day doing laundry and cleaning, trying not to worry about Anne. *God, lighten the load of my heart.* I went into the living room to do some dusting, then stopped abruptly.

I studied the Nativity scene. There were shepherds, along with the three wise men. The camels and sheep stood by Joseph, who gazed at Baby Jesus lying in the manger. Kneeling next to the babe was Mary.

Then it struck me. Where was Mary's family? I wondered what her mother's reaction had been when her pregnant daughter announced she was leaving home, departing on a donkey for faraway Bethlehem without a place to stay. Did she ask, "How can you just go? You need to be with your family at a time like this!" I wouldn't blame her if she had. But maybe she put her faith to work when her daughter set out on her journey, trusting God to guide and protect her. Mary's mother put her child's life in God's hands when her own were no longer enough.

That is the message of the crèche. That the Christ child came down to earth to be with us, to be part of our daily lives, our families. To let us know that God's presence will be there to strengthen and sustain us. It is ever present, even when families are apart. I ran my fingers over Mary's wooden shawl. I imagined Mary's mother's words: *You're in God's hands, my daughter. Go in peace.*

I had worried about Anne's being alone. Yet she hadn't been. The One who had been with us all in Connecticut had also been with Anne and her children hundreds of miles away. We had celebrated together after all.

Name of Jesus, heaven of gladness,
Cause our doubts and fears to cease;
Soothe away the aching sadness;
Name of Jesus, give us peace.
—AUTHOR UNKNOWN

LIVING IN THE NOW

by Bonnie Wheeler

I was strolling through the grounds of a local convent. In contrast to the beauty around me, I was grumbling and comparing the contrast between then and now:

> *Then* I was a full-time writer, teacher, speaker.
> *Now* I'm an accounting clerk.
> *Then* I traveled across the country.
> *Now* I spend my days trapped behind a desk.
> *Then* I spoke to hundreds.
> *Now* I work in a tiny office of four.
> *Then* I did work that mattered, ministry.
> *Now* . . .

At this point in my grousing, I came upon a statue of Jesus the Carpenter holding a simple piece of wood. I imagined those years before His public ministry, those simple years in Joseph's carpentry shop. Surely Jesus knew of His future ministry, of the throngs of people waiting so desperately for His healing touch, the wisdom only He could impart, the salvation only He could offer. Yet I couldn't imagine Jesus complaining to God about the boredom or insignificance of the carpenter's shop compared to the excitement and importance of the waiting ministry. I saw Jesus living in the *now*, striving to be the very best carpenter possible.

Monday morning found me not only refreshed, but committed to living in the *now*, to be the best I can be.

I long to rise in the arms of faith
And be closer drawn to thee.

—FANNY CROSBY

THE MERCY PRAYER

by Catherine Marshall

During a telephone chat, my friend Elaine was telling me about a christening she had just attended. "The baby being christened was not only crying but screaming," she said. "I could see how embarrassed the infant's parents were and I wanted to help them. So I prayed, 'Lord Jesus, have mercy on that baby and his father and mother.'

"Catherine, it was remarkable. The crying stopped immediately as if a faucet had been turned off."

I agreed that it was amazing, then added, "But, Elaine, the result doesn't surprise me as much as your particular petition."

"How so?"

"Oh, just that the 'have mercy' seems such an extreme request in a relatively mild situation. Most of us think of mercy as connected with a dire emergency. The word conjures up a mental picture of a condemned man standing before a judge pleading for pity."

Then Elaine explained how it had indeed been a dire emergency that had begun to reveal to her the many facets of God's mercy . . .

Eight years before, her husband Louis had undergone a serious cancer operation. He recovered and had been in good health until last summer when his doctor suspected a return of the cancer. "It was a time of great agony," Elaine told me. "All my reading of Scripture and praying—hours of it—led to a fresh realization of the unceasing compassion of a God of love.

"So my praying," she went on, "finally jelled into a single, heartfelt plea, 'Father in Heaven, will You have mercy on us simply for Jesus' sake?'"

The result? The cancer scare proved to be a false alarm.

But then Elaine went on to explain that, since then, God keeps showing her how He wants us to ask for and accept His mercy even in everyday things.

In the next few days, it was remarkable how passage after passage of Scripture to verify Elaine's Mercy Prayer was brought to my attention. I saw that many of Jesus' healings came as the result of a plea for mercy.

For instance, there were the two blind men sitting by the side of the road as Jesus was leaving Jericho (Matthew 20:29–34 KJV). Hearing that this was Jesus passing by, the two men cried out, "Have mercy on us, O Lord, Thou Son of David."

The crowd following the Master told them to keep quiet. But the blind men cried the louder, "Have mercy on us."

And Jesus, standing still and giving the men His full attention, asked what they wanted of Him. When they begged Jesus to open their eyes, He had compassion on them, touched the eyes of both men, and immediately each received his sight.

Then there was the time Jesus met ten lepers (Luke 17:11-19 AMP). Since lepers were ostracized from public gatherings, these men stood at a distance, crying, "Jesus, Master, take pity and have mercy on us."

The Master did not question each man about how well he had kept the Law or how righteous he was. Simply out of Jesus' overflowing, compassionate love, He healed them. "Go and show yourselves to the priests," He told them. And later, "Your faith has restored you to health."

Faith in what or in whom? The connecting link is our belief that God loves each of us with a love more wondrous than the most warmhearted person we know; that He heals simply out of His love and because He wants us to have the joy of abundant health. As the Apostle Paul put it: "Blessed be the God and Father of our Lord Jesus Christ, the Father of mercies and God of all comfort, who comforts us in all our affliction . . ." (2 Corinthians 1:3, 4 RSV).

In another place Paul tells us why Jesus did not inquire about the worthiness of those whom He healed or lifted out of sin: "So then (God's gift) is not a question of human will and human effort, but of God's mercy" (Romans 9:16 AMP). In other words, there is nothing you or I can do to earn God's gifts. We are dependent on His loving mercy. . . .

The insights about the Mercy Prayer were not over yet. During a wakeful time in the middle of the night, the inner Voice (there is no mistaking it!) forcibly reminded me of the particular words of the promise God had given me on the morning of Peter Marshall's death back in 1949. It had come as I had been about to leave the hospital room in which my husband's body lay. Even as I had reached for the doorknob, it was as if a firm hand had stopped me. Then, clearly and emphatically, yet with tenderness combined with surprising power, had come a line from Psalm 23:6 (KJV): "Goodness and mercy shall follow me all the days of my life."

And now, so many years later, deep in the night, the same Voice was saying, "Note that word *mercy*, Catherine. My goodness, My mercy. That's what is following you and will surround you to the end of your earthly walk. Lean back on that. Depend on it."

How needed that assurance was for me. . . . How needed for anyone in distress!

Who among us does not have needs in our troubled age? And to meet those needs, the resounding validity of the Mercy Prayer all through Scripture is meant for every one of us . . . "The Lord is good; his mercy is everlasting; and his truth endureth to all generations" (Psalm 100:5 KJV).

PRAYING IN OUR BEHALF

by Kathie Kania

There are times when I feel unable to pray effectively. My mind wanders; I feel as though I'm not "getting through." On a recent National Day of Prayer, I felt still more duty bound, as though my praying should be even more special, more powerful.

Then I came upon a quotation from Robert Murray McCheyne: "If I could hear Christ praying for me in the next room, I would not fear a million enemies. Yet distance makes no difference. He is praying for me."

Christ praying for me? Amazing! That thought is changing my whole perspective on prayer. I remember now that before He died, Christ prayed "for all who will believe in me" (John 17:20 NIV). That includes me. In that prayer, He asks that we'll all be as one, that we'll know He loves us. And He looks forward to our being with Him. And Hebrews 7:25 (KJV) describes Jesus in heaven: "He ever liveth to make intercession for them."

I guess I had been guilty of thinking that prayer was all on my shoulders. But with Christ praying for me, and the Spirit too, praying with "groans that words cannot express" (Romans 8:26 NIV), I'm finding that prayer is no longer a burden.

Yes, we are commanded to pray—in praise, in faith, in thanksgiving and with our requests. But isn't it comforting to know that even when we are weak and can't pray, the praying goes on—in our behalf. By the Mightiest.

IN THE FOURTH WATCH

by David Westerfield

Soft sunshine streamed through the skylight above me as foam cushions were placed on both sides of my head. Yellow plugs were inserted into my ears and I was told to lie still. Except for a strange electronic hum, the room was as quiet as it was sterile. I clenched my fists, then relaxed. My palms were moist and warm. With a sudden lurch the table I was on slid into a narrow white tunnel. The humming faded. The sunlight disappeared.

The Magnetic Resonance Imaging scanner is a diagnostic tool that can rule out surgery and even save lives. But at that moment, on a cool January day when I should have been opening the morning mail at work, the MRI was, for me, another mystery in a story that had been taking far too long to unfold.

I stared at the white wall of the cylinder six inches above my face. Then a knocking began, a pounding that told me the machine was making detailed images of my brain. I closed my eyes and wondered why such a sophisticated scanner had to sound like a jackhammer.

I wiggled my toes and tried to ignore the noise. I was getting the MRI because doctors were attempting to find out why I had been having severe head pain for the past six weeks. I was frightened; they were baffled. They had no idea what was going on. That's what scared me: the unknown.

The sudden pain had hit on a Monday morning. I was at the newspaper where I work, and my editor looked at me and asked, "Are you feeling okay, David?"

"I've got a bad headache. And I'm starting to get an upset stomach," I said in a tone that told her I was as puzzled as I was in pain. It was unusual for me; during the past ten years I had taken only two sick days. "I'm going out to my car to lie down for a while."

After a couple of hours I finally had to go home. I napped on the couch and went to bed earlier than usual. The next morning I was shaving when the pain returned. It was so intense I collapsed on the bed and called in sick later.

Soon I learned that if I stayed in bed or on the couch the pain was minimal. But if I got up for even a few minutes the headache grew unbearable and I became nauseated. On the fourth morning I saw our family physician and he gave me a shot to reduce the swelling in my head.

"We'll start with the most common cause for what you're experiencing and go from there. In medical school they taught us that if we hear hoofbeats to look for horses," he said. "The headaches you're having could be caused by a number of factors, even a brain tumor. But more likely they're due to a virus and that's how we're going to treat them."

Five weeks passed. I seemed to be getting better—I even managed to get out of the house. Then one Sunday morning those horses returned in full gallop. My wife Mareska was at church with our two children. I crawled to the couch as the hoofbeats pounded inside my head.

"Dear Lord, please take this pain away," I prayed as I half listened to a local pastor preach on television. "What is happening to me? What is going on? Dear God, whatever it is, please make me better."

I heard no answers to my questions, but within an hour the pain had eased enough for me to watch the football play-offs on TV. The next morning I called my family doctor, who was surprised to hear I hadn't recovered yet.

He sent me to a specialist, who ordered the MRI. From the results we learned there was swelling in the lining around my brain and a pocket of fluid on the left side of my head, but the MRI didn't tell us what had caused any of this. I was admitted to a hospital.

A spinal tap drew fluid from around my spinal column. It showed an abnormally high level of protein, a possible reaction to whatever had caused the swelling. Blood tests were done. X-rays were taken. Neurological exams and skin tests were performed. More blood was drawn.

Two days later I was sent into the MRI scanner again for a look at the blood vessels in my head. I was relieved, if not relaxed, when I was wheeled back to my room on the ninth floor.

But we were no closer to a diagnosis than we had been six weeks earlier. And I still couldn't stay on my feet for more than fifteen to twenty minutes at a time. *What if I had a rare virus that couldn't be treated? What if it killed me?*

All these worries were running through my mind when our pastor, David Newell, walked into my hospital room. He had been a faithful friend and prayer partner; more than once he had asked God to heal me.

We talked about the hospital room and the weather and some special services planned at the church that weekend. Then he took a deep breath and seemed to stand a bit taller. "I'm reminded of the disciples the night they were in the boat without Jesus. He had gone up the mountain to pray and had sent them on ahead." Pastor Dave told the story as though he had been there himself.

"Strong winds came up and the waves got rough. The disciples were frightened. They wondered why Jesus had sent them out into the rough seas. Some of them were filled with doubts. Were they about to die?"

Pastor Dave pulled me into his hospital-room sermon as though he were pulling me onto that boat. He was speaking of the disciples—and he was speaking of me.

"Jesus could have kept that boat out of the storm. Or he could have made the storm blow in another direction. But He didn't do that. He had something for the disciples to learn that night. And they had to learn it in the midst of the storm. When the disciples really needed Him, He came. In the fourth watch.

"Remember that, David. Jesus comes in the fourth watch. When the night seems darkest. When the waves are at their highest. When we are the most afraid and confused."

Then Pastor Dave placed his hands—as warm as if they had been close to a fire—on my head and chest and started to pray. "Fear not!" he nearly shouted. "Fear not!" The two words I needed to hear most.

Lord, I prayed, *give me peace.*

Later that day the doctors decided to release me. Ever so slowly the pain went away and the nausea left me. Gradually I regained my strength. Twelve weeks after my mystery illness struck, I returned to work.

All of this happened two years ago, and the headaches have never returned. Sometimes people ask, "Don't you wonder about it? Wouldn't you feel better if the doctors had found out exactly what it was?"

I tell them that I know all I need to know. Once I was mysteriously ill; today I am well. When the night was darkest, when I entered the fourth watch, Jesus was there.

MY WORRY WINDOW

by Sue Monk Kidd

In a church where I once belonged, there was a particular stained glass window that always drew my attention. It simply portrayed Christ standing with His hands held opened together in front of Him.

One Sunday I was sitting in church feeling the heaviness of a problem that had been troubling me for some time. My eyes were drawn to the stained glass window once more. The figure of Christ holding His hands cupped in front of Him seemed to be waiting for someone to drop something into them. I stared at the opened hands. *Give it to Me,* the scene seemed to whisper. And in that moment I imagined myself reaching inside me and lifting a heavy stone of worry from within and placing it into the Hands in the window—the waiting Hands of Christ. And as I did, I felt a sudden lightness . . . the freedom that comes only from releasing our burdens and trusting them to God. The problem I had been carrying did not immediately resolve itself, but my heart was now freed to find a creative solution I had not seen before.

From that day forward, that window became my "worry window"—a place to which I could come and leave my fears and anxieties every week . . . a place that helped me learn to let go and trust.

Maybe there is an open pair of Hands waiting to receive your burden right now.

PART 8

Glimpses of Jesus as Mentor and Model

MONTHS AFTER JESUS' RESURRECTION AND ASCENSION, Peter succinctly summarized Jesus' earthly ministry. "He went around doing good . . ." Acts 10:38 (NIV). As a teenager I sang a church duet that included this verse and then continued, "like him we should be."

Being like Jesus. It's the desire behind the question "What would Jesus do?"—a question that comes up in several stories in this section. As shown in Scripture, His actions, conversations and teachings provide a model for us to live by.

Maybe it's time for you and me, like John Sherrill, to put on our "Jesus Shoes" and walk life's path with Him.

JESUS' FIRST AND LAST PRAYER

by Scott Walker

The first prayer my mother taught me was the bedtime one that begins "Now I lay me down to sleep, I pray the Lord my soul to keep." American children by the thousands have begun their prayer life with these simple and beautiful words.

The Jews of the ancient world also had a first prayer that they taught their children. It ended with these words: "Father, into Thy hands I commit my spirit." I discovered this fact when I was doing some background reading on the death of Jesus. The prayer Jesus breathed with His final gasp of life was the simple one Mary had taught Him as a little boy. At that poignant realization, I felt tears running down my cheeks.

In the weeks since this discovery, I have adopted a new custom. On those days when life is hard and everything is closing in on me—like the stress of work commitments and, recently, my wife's cancer scare—I walk into my room and flop down on my bed. With arms outstretched, I lie there for a few moments and consciously feel the mattress support my body and the pillow cradle my head. Then I slowly breathe the words of Jesus, "Father, into Thy hands I commit my spirit."

Every time I do this, I feel supported by the presence of God. I know that my Father does hold my life in His hands and will not let go. I rediscover a childlike faith and I am no longer afraid of the dark.

JESUS' PRAYER PRIORITIES

by Elizabeth Sherrill

As I was saying the Lord's Prayer several years ago, I was struck by two words: *Give us*. How late in the prayer it comes, this very first request for our own needs—halfway to the end! Since the words Jesus gave His disciples were the pattern for the entire life of prayer, He must have been telling them, "Your own needs must always come second."

That certainly hadn't been my order of business! My prayers usually led off with a cry for help: "*Give* me the words to write her," when Maude's husband died. "*Protect* Andrew on his trip." "*Guide* the doctors during Fran's surgery."

Jesus has different priorities. Start by honoring God, He tells me. Hallow His name. Pray for His kingdom. Seek His will. Spend half your prayer time—the first half—putting the Father first. Jesus was all too aware of the wrenching human need He was sending His disciples to confront. Yet He didn't tell them, "Here's how to ask for God's aid in difficult situations." He said, "Worship God."

So I set out to follow this model. It is a tough discipline when the need is urgent! The very first week of the experiment, the prayer chain at our church learned of a college student—a parishioner's daughter—threatening suicide. *Make her answer her mother's phone calls, God!* I wanted to cry. *Have the dorm staff force open her door! Get her boyfriend to apologize!*

Instead, using the sequence of the Lord's Prayer, I made myself start not with the problem but with God's all-sufficiency. I concentrated on the greatness of His name. I asked for His kingdom to come everywhere on earth, including that dorm room; for His will to be done in all situations, not this one alone.

And as I followed Jesus' pattern, a curious thing happened. The panic was gone. I found myself offering my intercessions while focusing on the nature of God, forever working toward the very best. The prayers of many people were in fact answered when the student at last picked up the telephone and spoke to her mother.

Looking at our need through the lens of God's love: That must be why, in the prayer Jesus taught, the words *Give us* come so late.

*"The good man brings
good things out of the good
stored up in his heart. . . ."*

—LUKE 6:45 (NIV)

HIS YOKE IS EASY

by Kathie Kania

I nearly broke my neck getting to my place at the piano bench just before the Sunday morning service began. *Day of rest?* I thought. *Not quite.* I'd been rushing around since I got out of bed.

Michael and our young girls, Kristin and Breton, had raved about my new blueberry pancake recipe, but I had to excuse myself from the breakfast table because I needed to get organized for Sunday school. Somehow I'd wound up with the pre-K class that met in the half hour before the service. "Kathie, you're overextending yourself," Michael had warned when I accepted the post. I threw together a lesson plan, then got the girls ready for church. "Where's your other dress shoe, Kristin?" "Breton, you have a Cheerio in your hair!" All that before I faced a roomful of three-year-olds who had glued more construction paper to their clothes than to the poster board I'd brought. How was I ever supposed to teach them the Bible?

Now I barely had a chance to catch my breath at the piano before the minister introduced the first hymn. As my fingers hit the opening notes of "All for Jesus," my mind drifted from him to the many projects on my plate. "All for What?" was the tune playing in my heart. I could hardly remember the key for the next hymn, and when our pastor gave his message I was only half listening. Something about Jesus saying, "My yoke is easy, my burden is light." *Not from where I'm sitting,* I thought. I wished I could be let in on the secret.

After the service I went to untangle my girls from the crowd of kids outside. "C'mon, Kristin, Breton." One of the mothers caught me by surprise. "I'm so glad I bumped into you, Kathie. Banners," she said over her shoulder, while she shepherded off her children. "For the Bible club. Can you have them ready by Wednesday?"

I heard myself saying yes almost before my brain had processed the request. "By Wednesday for sure," I said. How could I say no? I was an artist and a cartoonist, and I taught painting. People were always asking me to do community art projects, and I was glad to help.

"Let's go, girls. Now." Something in my voice made them snap to. We headed for the car and buckled ourselves in. My foot hit the gas. "Mom," Breton said from the backseat, "who are you so mad at?"

"I'm just tired," I said, slowing down, "and I have a lot to do." I was also confused. *Lord, the more I try to follow you, to serve you by helping others, the more drained I feel.* Something wasn't right.

At home I grabbed the school directory and got right on my bedroom phone. I'd volunteered to enlist chaperones for an upcoming field trip. Of course, I was going myself, as usual. I dialed the first number, starting with the A's.

Well into the D's, and without much success, I flopped back on my pillows. *This will take longer than I thought.* One of my best paintings hung on the wall across the room from me—Main Street in my hometown, after a summer rain. Though I had done it years ago, I recalled vividly the thrill of painting it. I had dreamed of bringing this serene scene to life. Portraiture came more naturally to me, and this was slow going. But it didn't ever seem burdensome; the extra effort only made the finished work more fulfilling for me. Eventually I completed an entire hometown series.

Michael came in and caught me daydreaming. "Ahh," he said, "what do we have here? A moment to yourself?" He sat down next to me. "I'm worried about you." He pointed to the painting on the wall. "You're so busy, you're not painting like you used to. And I kind of miss the ragtag bunch of artistes passing through the house all the time. Such determination—sometimes more determination than talent!" I laughed. "But you know how to get the best out of them," he said.

"Remember Jeannie?" I asked.

"Sure," Michael said. "The horse-head artist. How could I forget?"

Jeannie had lugged her oils, easel and brushes to my studio once a week. How she labored over her paintings, each one perfect in terms of technique, but still flat somehow. "I hope this is what Aunt Sarah had in mind," she'd say, sighing, or, "My husband said to be sure to put a red barn in the field." She constantly second-guessed herself instead of trusting her own instincts. I gave her a lot of pointers on color and composition, but I didn't know how to inspire her. Something was missing not from the canvas but from the artist herself. "I should do something for my sister," Jeannie said one week. "She likes bright colors."

"Jeannie!" I fairly shouted. "What about you? What do you want to paint?"

Jeannie thought about it. "I have an old note card with four Arabian horse heads on it," she said. "One day I'd like to paint a copy of it on a huge canvas."

"We'll stretch the canvas next week. Bring your picture."

Over the coming weeks she worked with almost no help from me. The buttery colors she blended showed off the gorgeous muscles in the horses' necks. Their bold eyes drew you into the picture. A wisp of mane blew in an imaginary wind. This painting stood apart from everything else she had done.

Michael sat down next to me on the bed. "She found her talent when she found herself," he said.

"Paint what you love, I always say. Not what you think you should."

"Might that go for 'doing' too? As in, Do what you love, not what you think you should do—which, as far as I can tell from your constant volunteering, seems to be everything."

"I just want to do my part. People expect it. Jesus expects it. It's all for him."

"Are you sure? Or is it just a little bit for you, and what people think of you?"

Michael made me stop and take a good, hard look at myself. I did want people to think well of me, to say, "Wow, what a fine person Kathie is. Look at how she serves the Lord." Was that so wrong? But the truth was, I was burning out. I didn't feel inspired. I wasn't being honest with my neighbors or myself when I pretended I could take on yet another project. Jesus deserved my best, and I was making it impossible to give it to him. In a way, I was painting other people's paintings, just like Jeannie had done. "Thanks, Michael," I said and hopped off the bed.

I was determined to show my true colors, no matter what people thought of me. I developed a game plan. From now on, I would simply pick and choose, thoughtfully, the best way to do my part. That afternoon I signed up one extra chaperone for the school field trip—to take my place for once. Then I stopped doing every banner and art project in the entire community just because I had a creative streak. In fact, some real talent came forward when I started saying no. New talent showed itself in our kitchen too. Michael learned to make some serious blueberry pancakes.

Funny thing is, I'm not doing a whole lot less volunteering than I was before. But when I play "All for Jesus" at the piano, I play honestly and passionately, because I've chosen how to serve Him best. That is the secret of the easy yoke.

HOLY TERROR

by B. G. Brown

When he first moved in next door, he was a screaming baby. Four years later he was still next door, a permanent fixture in the otherwise serene Lonesome Pines subdivision where I had lived a quiet suburban life for twenty years.

Michael, short for his age, had blond curly hair and a disarming pug nose. Long dark lashes framed his inscrutable blue eyes. To avoid boredom, Michael stayed busy—annoying me. A generation earlier cartoonist Hank Ketcham could have used Michael and me as his inspiration: Michael playing Dennis the Menace to my Mr. Wilson.

Returning from a trip one day, I unloaded my car and walked around to check my prized navel orange tree. It was going to produce a bumper crop this year, and I was anxious to see if any fruit had ripened. But when I turned the corner of the house, I froze. Dozens of green oranges littered the ground. A little detective work revealed that whoever had yanked them off was short: The only oranges left on the tree were four feet and above.

Michael's seven-year-old sister Laura ran over to the fence between our houses. "Mr. Brown," she asked with a mischievous smile, "do you want to know who pulled the oranges off your tree?"

"I sure do."

"It was Michael!"

I phoned his mother. "Linda, Laura told me Michael pulled the oranges off my tree. I thought you'd want to know."

In a few moments, the doorbell rang. Linda held Michael with an iron grip. "Go on, Michael," she prompted. Through tears and clenched teeth, Michael managed to choke out, "I'm sorry."

"You're forgiven," I replied, my voice cold as steel. "Just don't do it again."

He obeyed—at least as far as oranges were concerned. He next turned to grapefruit. I discovered them scattered all over my backyard, thrown from the tree in his own yard. Now I was mad! I called Linda again. "Most of the grapefruit from your tree is lying in my backyard!" This elicited another apology from the little demon, even more coerced than before.

For a few days we had peace, so I thought Michael had learned his lesson. And then . . .

Bang! I ran to the front door. My sloping driveway had become Michael's Grand Prix racetrack. Pushing his three-wheeler up to my garage door, he'd stand up and ram it backward to make use of every possible inch for a speedier, longer ride.

"Don't hit the garage door! See the black marks you're leaving?" I bellowed in my best Mr. Wilson yell. Michael turned and stared at me defiantly, then zoomed away.

After that Michael made himself scarce. My hopes soared . . . maybe the war was over. Then one broiling day I turned on the sprinkler just enough to cover one small section of my lawn. Back inside, I settled down to work. Suddenly I heard the water pressure surge. Rushing outside, I saw the water spraying like a geyser over the yard, the driveway, the roof! As I rushed to turn off the faucet, I got soaked. Naturally.

Michael was in his bathing suit, blissfully playing in a puddle. "Michael!" I thundered. "Don't do that again!"

I was still fuming the next day when I came home from shopping and unloaded some cantaloupes onto my garage floor. Michael and Laura bounded over to check out what was going on, and Michael promptly headed for the cantaloupes and pounded one with his plastic bat. "Son," I snapped, "don't hit the cantaloupes."

"I'm not your son!" he announced firmly. Good thing you're not, I thought. Enough of this spare-the-rod business. I wanted to put him over my knee.

When the Christmas holidays came, my wife and I spent two wonderful weeks in Missouri with our daughter and her family. Michael couldn't harass me 1,300 miles away. *Maybe moving to Missouri would solve the problem,* I thought on the plane home.

Over the holidays I had read the book *Joshua* by Joseph F. Girzone. The title character was a contemporary Jesus—a gentle, patient man who loved children. They loved him in return and followed him wherever he went. I felt as if God had been speaking to me through the book about my own relationship with my young tormentor. "The problem is that you don't love Michael," He seemed to say. "But, Lord," I countered, "you wouldn't love him if you had to live next door to him." God didn't buy my argument; He kept giving me nudges. I didn't want to love Michael, and didn't particularly want God to either. Finally a verse of Scripture crossed my mind: For it is God which worketh in you both to will and to do of his good pleasure (Philippians 2:13 KJV). I knew God would show me how to love Michael if I allowed Him. "Okay, Lord," I said. "I'm willing to try."

When we got home, I stepped out the side door of my garage to check the yard. There sat Michael on the small top bar of the chain-link fence, looking like a cat ready to pounce.

"Hi, Michael," I said, smiling. "Did you have a nice Christmas?"

He tottered on the fence, apparently shocked that I was speaking to him in a pleasant tone of voice.

A feeling prompted me. "Michael, what did you get for Christmas?" I asked. To my surprise he described each toy excitedly.

I started to walk away when from behind me piped a friendly voice I barely recognized. "Mr. Brown, what did you get for Christmas?"

I turned. His stare wasn't blank anymore; his eyes were alive. I felt myself soften. He smiled; I smiled back. I told him about my Christmas in Missouri. I even took him into the garage to see some new tools I had gotten.

During the months that followed, Michael and I became friends. We played Frisbee and puttered in my garage. He told me about his kindergarten girlfriend and how he planned to marry her when he grew up.

Michael is no longer my tormentor. He's my lovable next-door neighbor. Dennis the Menace seems to be gone for good.

And Mr. Wilson no longer lives at my house.

*All the way from earth to glory,
I would be like Jesus.*
—JAMES ROWE

THAT "LITTLE INSTRUCTION BOOK"

by H. Jackson Brown Jr.

I sat slumped in our family room staring at the wall, miserable over what I had done to my fifteen-year-old son. Our relationship had not been the best through the years, and this evening I had really blown it. Adam had not gone out for his high-school football team as I had strongly urged, and I had sounded off about it to him.

"Golly, I'm sorry, Dad," he had said, his brown eyes full of hurt, "but I was more interested in the Computer Club."

"If that's the way you want it," I growled, picking up the newspaper to let him know our talk was over.

Adam trudged upstairs to his room, and I sank back in my chair, letting the paper fall to the floor. I was piqued that my advice had been disregarded, and frustrated at not having a closer relationship with our only child.

It seemed to have been this way since Adam was little. I remembered him sitting behind me in the car as I drove home from a local swimming pool. Despite all my instructions, he had not swum as well as I wished. When we stopped at a light, I scolded him: "Adam, you disappointed me! I took you over there because you said you were going to swim like a big boy with your face in the water. But you're still fearful. I'm angry at you."

His face puckered. "Daddy, it makes me sad when you talk to me like that."

It was as if an arrow had pierced my heart. *Better get hold of yourself, Jackson,* I thought at the time. You're talking to a five-year-old as if he's fifteen. Now, ten years later, I realized I had been talking to a fifteen-year-old as if he were five.

I shook my head, got up and climbed the stairs to Adam's room. I knocked softly on his door. "Adam?"

A muffled, "What?"

"I'm sorry," I said. "I shouldn't have talked to you like that."

"Yeah, Dad, yeah . . . no problem."

I turned to our bedroom knowing I had failed again. I realized I was trying to relive my youth through Adam, and when he didn't seem to listen, I flew off the handle, hurling words before I had a chance to think about them. The momentary satisfaction of venting my anger cost me days of trying to pick up the pieces of our broken relationship.

I loved Adam, wanted the best for him. But I knew the day would come when those pieces wouldn't be there to pick up anymore. Already I sensed a growing gulf between us.

Would I always be haunted by this dark side, I wondered, these volcanic outbursts?

Some days later while walking in downtown Nashville, I was thinking of the terrible role model I had become. Kids may not do what you tell them to do, but they are watching you all the time. I knew you couldn't tell a child not to smoke if you smoked, or not to drink if you drank. What was Adam seeing in me?

Then something caught my eye. It was a big sign in the window of a shoe shop. I stopped and looked at it:

CLOSED FOR REMODELING

Opening Soon Under
New Management

The message hit me like a lightning bolt. Could I remodel myself and open under new management? I brought it up in conversation with an old minister friend, Brad Sprague.

"What can I do, Brad?" I asked.

Looking at me through his glasses, he quietly asked, "What would Christ do?"

What had He done? I thought of the biblical accounts of the times Jesus had been baited, insulted and vilified. Any ordinary person would have exploded, but His calm, measured responses always put things into perspective. I determined to put my reactions under His control.

In the weeks following, I tried, but I found that my tendency to blow up had become second nature, a reflex. I remembered something I learned in a college psychology class: The best way to end a bad habit is to replace it with a good one. So when I sensed an eruption coming on, I'd hold my tongue for some seconds while I breathed deeply. Usually the anger would dissipate. It wasn't easy at first. But I found that when one resists the devil, he will flee (James 4:7).

In the beginning Adam looked at me warily. But gradually he relaxed, and it wasn't long before we had some fairly decent conversations. The more we talked, the more I realized Adam's uniqueness in his own abilities. He was a computer whiz, and before long he was helping me adapt computer techniques to my business.

A big step forward came about eleven o'clock one night when Adam returned from a date. Instead of going right up to his room as usual, he came into the family room, sat down and began to chat.

Saturdays became a special time for us. We drove to different county seats to try out restaurants with a culinary claim to fame, such as chicken-fried steak or chocolate meringue pie. I knew I was making real progress when Adam asked, "Gee, Dad, where are we going next week?"

In launching my self-remodeling project, I also found help in reading material and listening to tapes, not only of Scripture but by persons who had found spiritually fulfilling lives. I discovered so many helpful insights that I began collecting them, augmenting them with my own.

Then as the time approached for Adam to leave for college, I began to wonder: *What could I give that he could take with him? What about my new collection of wisdom?* I retreated to the family room to copy down some of the insights and observations I thought he might find useful.

That first night I wrote down forty-one thoughts in a notebook, beginning with: *Compliment three people every day* and ending with *Don't postpone joy.* What I thought would take a few hours took several days as I added more: *Be kinder than necessary* and *Give yourself a year and read the Bible cover to cover.* Number ninety-three came when I thought about my wife Rosemary. I wrote: *Choose your life's mate carefully. From this one decision will come ninety percent of all your happiness or misery.*

Rosemary helped with the collection, typing the instructions as I wrote them. The night before Adam was to leave, I had 511 reminders; the last was *Call your mother.*

I assembled the typed pages in a dime-store binder and slid it under the front seat of our station wagon. The next day, as his mother and I helped him move into his dorm room, I reached under the car seat, pulled out the binder and handed it to him.

"Adam, this is what I know about living a happy and rewarding life."

"Thanks, Dad," he exclaimed, and we hugged good-bye.

About a week later Adam called. He told me that he cherished the book. He was going to continue it, he said, adding some of his own thoughts, and someday pass it on to his child.

It was a high point of my life. Perhaps in some small way entry 508 in that little book was coming true: Become someone's hero.

Editor's note: H. Jackson Brown Jr.'s book of suggestions became the national best-seller Life's Little Instruction Book, *published in 1991 by Rutledge Hill Press, Nashville, Tennessee.*

More like the Master I would live and grow;
More of his love to others I would show.

—CHARLES H. GABRIEL

THE CALL I DIDN'T MAKE

by Ernest Shubird

I was more than ready for the workweek to end. Because of recent legislation, our office had been required to change the way local administrators applied for operating funds. As a state administrator for vocational education, I was the one who prepared and sent out the new application packages, and I was exhausted.

Ten minutes before it was time to go home on Friday, my phone rang. It was one of the local administrators, whom I'll call B.J. "Doc," he snapped, "I've just tried to read these applications you've sent out, and I'm confused as a blind cow in a rail pile. I'd like to know who wrote this thing." After a minute-long tirade, he paused long enough for me to get a word in. "Hold on, B.J.," I said. "Why not let this rest until Monday? We can discuss it then."

"I should have known I wouldn't get any help from your office," he snarled. The phone clicked. He had hung up.

Every time I thought of B.J. that weekend, I fumed. I had worked long and hard on the wording of those applications. Who did he think he was, blasting off at me? My reputation is at stake, I told myself—and I intended to blast him right back. One thing was certain: I'd get back to B.J.—and if he still took issue with the applications, he could forget about receiving any funds in the near future.

On Monday morning I sat at my office phone ready to confront him. But after dialing his number, I quickly hung up.

Why couldn't I go ahead? After all, he deserved any reprimands I might throw at him. I picked up the phone again. *Okay, B.J., it's time to let you have it.* I dialed. After one ring a question came to mind: *What would Jesus do in this situation?* I replaced the receiver. I knew what he would not do.

The phone rang. It was B.J. I barely had time to say hello when he started in again—this time in a mellow voice. "Doctor Shubird," he began, "I'm sorry I ran my big mouth off on Friday. I had just had three upset parents in my office, and problems with a teacher—more than I could stand. Now that I've settled down, I'd like to talk about these applications."

Silently I said a thankful prayer—for the call I didn't make. My reputation had been at stake—in more ways than one. "It's okay, B.J.," I said. "I have plenty of time for you. I'm here to help."

HE POINTED HER TO
THE LIVING WATER

by Dorothy Shellenberger

I am particularly drawn to Jesus' words, "And he must needs go through Samaria," and the encounter with the Samaritan woman that follows. This scene and Jesus' words speak to me in a special way because of an experience in my own life.

Not long ago a call came to me from a woman in Montgomery, Alabama. She had sat next to a physician friend of ours at a dinner party, and as people so often do, she had asked him for medical advice about her daughter who was temporarily living in our city. The doctor told her that he had friends there and gave the woman my name.

In desperation she called and asked if I would please check on her daughter who had been sick, was jobless, and had no car, telephone or friends. In response to this woman's cry for help I told her I would go see her daughter.

When I drove to the address that had been given me, I discovered it was on a sleazy, run-down street where neglected apartments are sandwiched in between topless bars. Like the Jews of Jesus' day, I would gladly have gone miles out of my way to avoid being seen after sunup on Third Street.

As I stopped in front of a nondescript house that was badly in need of paint, two thoughts raced through my mind: *What in the world am I doing here?* And, *I hope she isn't home—then I can just leave a note.* But she was home, and I was trapped.

We sat on her porch and talked. I gave her a jar of homemade apple-sauce; she thanked me and said she hadn't eaten all day.

The next day I took her grocery shopping.

Yesterday I took her to the Family Clinic for a physical checkup. Her bravado broke down on the way home. As tears poured down her cheeks, she told me how scared she was. I held her in my arms for a long time.

It would be easy to condemn her. Her straw-colored hair showed an inch of darkened roots, her heavy makeup was ineptly applied, and her boisterous, flirty manner bugled a lifestyle that I don't approve of. But slowly I began to see that berating her and writing her off would be tanta-mount to the behavior of the judgmental legalists of Jesus' day, whom He repeatedly chastised. To follow in His way means to practice His presence. And practicing His presence means showing the gentle, healing love that Jesus showed the Samaritan woman as He pointed her to the "living water."

Tomorrow I'm taking Jo some stationery, but not the kind she asked me for. "Just any old stuff," she'd said. "I don't even care if the envelopes match, but I need to write my mom. I know she is worried about me." Somehow Jo needs to know that she is worth a lot more than a pretty box of stationery with matching envelopes, but that is a start.

Perhaps too tomorrow will be the day that we will get beyond her sur-face problems and she will find the living water that Jesus so lovingly offered to the woman at the well . . . and that He still offers to my new-found friend on Third Street.

WHEN I LOOK ONLY TO JESUS

by Muriel Leeson

I had just come from a meeting at church when I saw my husband in the yard building the picket fence we'd been planning. I went out to keep him company. While he meticulously measured, then sawed dozens of pointed stakes, I talked—or raved, really—about the virtues of one of our church leaders. "Now there's a real Christian," I said. "She's someone I wish I could be like. In fact, she'd be a good model for me to follow."

My husband did not look up from his work as he asked quietly, "Wouldn't you do better to pattern yourself after the original?"

"The original what?" I said, perplexed.

"The original Christian," he replied. Then he held up a stake he had just completed. "Look, you'll notice that I have cut every picket the same length, but I've never used the last one sawed as a measuring guide. I always go back to the first picket because if I don't, each time I'll pick up a slight error and eventually that error will be magnified. No, the original is the true guide."

I saw his point. None of us human beings is perfect, but God's Son is. When I look only to Jesus, I will neither expect too much from a brother nor unconsciously reproduce his mistakes.

THE JESUS SHOES

by John Sherrill

I lay in a hospital bed, disconsolate and more than a little bored. Doctors said I would be there for ten days while they tried to diagnose my abdominal pain. The discomfort was mostly gone now, and I was more than ready to go home.

At 4:00 AM I was roused by a nurse checking my temperature and blood pressure. Unable to get back to sleep, I decided to take a walk. So, tethered to an IV pole, I made my way along the deserted corridor, my aluminum caddy rattling beside me on its tiny wheels, my Birkenstock sandals flopping on the tile floor.

At the nurses' desk was a young woman at her computer. On my earlier walks she had not even glanced up, but now she turned from the screen and smiled.

"Here comes the man in the Jesus shoes," she said.

I laughed for the first time in days. "Jesus shoes?"

"That's my husband's name for Birkenstocks," she explained. I looked down at the sturdy brown sandals with the broad bands of leather across my feet; indeed they did look like the shoes you see in paintings of Jesus and the Disciples.

We talked for a few minutes. She told me she had been working fourteen hours nonstop: She and her husband both worked overtime just to make ends meet. Feeling less sorry for myself, I resumed my walk. With my sandals clomping along beneath me I wondered if I could turn the long days in the hospital into a unique experience . . . unobtrusively walk in Jesus' footsteps while my own life got back to normal.

From that day on, I walked the halls of Northern Westchester Hospital in a different mood. Most of the time I did not talk about God or pray aloud with people, but I always prayed silently. And I listened with new attentiveness. It was astonishing how often doctors and nurses, other patients, visitors, volunteers and cleaning staff would bring up personal matters as I walked in my Jesus shoes.

Of course, the difference was interior. Instead of focusing on my own woes, I became concerned—like Jesus—with other people. Today, long after the doctors released me from the hospital with nothing more than a change in diet, I still think of those sandals as my Jesus shoes. When I'm feeling sorry for myself I put them on, even if only in my imagination, recalling the night a young woman at a computer console looked up and said, "Here comes the man in the Jesus shoes."

· PART 9 ·

Glimpses of Jesus as Our Strength for the Journey

FOOD AND WATER, THEY'RE THE ESSENTIAL ELEMENTS for sustaining strength on a long walk. Spiritually we find those empowering, nutritional properties in Jesus. On one occasion he said he was the "bread of life" (John 6:35). On another day he said, "If anyone is thirsty, let him come to me and drink" (John 7:37 NIV).

How did the apostle Paul summarize the power given him by Jesus? "I can do all things through Christ which strengtheneth me" (Philippians 4:13 KJV). His claim is central to the stories in this section, starting with the dramatic dream of Rulon Gardner on the day he learned how Jesus' strength could bolster his physically compromised condition.

Other writers in this section offer insights into how a spiritual strength is given and appropriated: through Scripture, through a symbolic breaking of bread, through holding onto the promise and awareness of Christ's love.

Come further along on this journey with Jesus. . . .

LORD, I AM WEAK AND
YOU ARE STRONG

by Rulon Gardner

All my life, it seems, folks have been telling me what I can't do. In school, my learning disability kept me from picking up things as quickly as the other students. On the playground, I was the biggest, slowest kid. No one thought I could ever be an athlete—except for my mom and dad, who were always telling me that with prayer and persistence I could find the strength to do anything.

Maybe that's why I was always pushing myself. I found a sport where my 286 pounds were an asset, wrestling, and I took it all the way to the Sydney Olympics in 2000. Naturally I was the underdog, but I made it to the final round and faced the best in the world, the legendary Russian Alexander Karelin, undefeated in fourteen years of competition. I had an older brother Ronald who died when I was eight. I'd win this medal for him. "Rulon doesn't stand a chance," the commentators said. "He might as well go home before he gets hurt." I stood alone on the mat and looked Karelin in the eye. You can do it! I shouted at myself silently. And I did. I beat him. I came back to my parents' farm in Afton, Wyoming, with a gold medal and the champion's belt.

I'd reached the pinnacle, right? But no, I kept looking for new challenges, for other ways to show the world, "Look what I can do!" Afton, in

Star Valley, where the Grand Tetons taper into the wooded peaks of the Salt River Range, was just the place for it. I gunned my Jeep around mountain curves, the closer to the edge the better. I raced my four-wheeler through the forests. I pulled stunts with my snowmobile on frozen lakes. I was always testing my limits—and maybe those of the people around me too.

February 14, 2002, I did my morning workout, then met up with my buddies Danny and Trent for a big lunch. It was about twenty-five degrees, and the winter sunlight sparkled on the deep snowdrifts that blanketed Afton. "Perfect day for snowmobiling," I said, pushing my empty plate away. "We've got four more hours of sunlight. Who wants to have some fun?" We got our gear and by 1:30 we were roaring through the woods, taking deep gulps of cold air and letting civilization disappear behind us as we climbed into the mountains on our snowmobiles.

Around 3:30, Danny said he'd had enough. "Gotta go. Can't miss my daughter's basketball game. Call me later." Trent mentioned heading in too. "Are you kidding, man?" I exploded. "We've still got to tackle Wagner Mountain!"

I revved my motor and shot uphill. The snowmobile slid and I braced with my feet. At the top, I looked over my shoulder for Trent. He was nowhere to be seen. *I guess he gave up,* I thought. *I'll just take a look around before I turn back.* I'd never been up here before. I explored the ridge, loving the spectacular view of Star Valley spreading out below. I called Danny on my cell phone. "I'm on top of the world!" I shouted. "I'll get Trent and head down in a few minutes. Let's meet for dinner after the game."

I swigged the last of my Gatorade and turned back. I found Trent's tracks and followed them. It was 4:30 now. The sun had started to dip under the ridgeline, casting long shadows on the snow. *Man, these are my tracks,* I realized, *not Trent's!* I took out my cell phone to call him, but now that I was off the peak, I couldn't get a signal.

I wasn't far from the Salt River, which winds down into Star Valley, carving a deep gully in the mountainside. *I'll bet he's checking out the gully,* I thought. Its slopes were awesome for snowmobiles. I drove down into the gully. No sign of Trent. *The river flows back to Afton,* I thought. *Might as well follow it home. Trent'll get back on his own.*

I rode alongside the river. A couple places it had overflowed, making semifrozen waterholes. I tried to cross one. The ice cracked and the rear end of the snowmobile sank underwater. I jumped out, feet soaked. No problem. I could get my snowmobile out. Those things weigh about six hundred pounds, but I was strong. I pulled until the sweat was steaming off me. It didn't budge. I broke off a big tree branch and levered the machine out, and started on my way again.

Another waterhole. Same thing happened, except I ended up soaked to my thighs. Better stick to the slope.

It was pitch-dark by now, but I figured I was entering Star Valley. I was bound to see a road soon, then Afton would be a clear shot. I imagined a big steak dinner waiting with a tall glass of Mountain Dew. My stomach rumbled.

The river narrowed and the sides of the gully steepened to almost vertical. I can't get up that—better just keep going. I inched forward, sending rocks and dirt tumbling under me. Suddenly my snowmobile skidded and slid straight down the slope into the river. I picked myself up, unhurt, but soaked, and stared at the snowmobile on its side in the water. This time I wouldn't be hauling it out.

The wind cut straight through the fleece jacket I was wearing. Underneath, I had a sweatshirt, T-shirt and runner's tights—fine for an afternoon ride, but no match for a night in the wild. I shivered. I could hear the water sloshing in my boots, but I couldn't feel my toes. I tried to take off the boots so I could wring out my socks. My fingers were so cold I couldn't undo the laces. There was a grove of trees nearby. I struggled through waist-deep snow to take shelter.

Still no signal on my cell phone. The clock showed 7:30. Danny and Trent know I wouldn't miss dinner. I'll just wait here till they come back for me. I kicked the snow from under a tree and sat down. I felt sore and tired like I'd just wrestled ten matches in a row. All I wanted to do was sleep. That's your body shutting down, hypothermia taking over. "Stay awake, Rulon!" I shouted at myself.

I stood up, sat down, pinched myself. I checked my cell phone again: 8:30. *What's keeping those guys?* I dozed off, then jerked awake. "Get up! Keep moving!" I yelled again, just like I did on the wrestling mat. But it was no use. One minute I'd be staring up at the bright stars overhead, the next I would wake up spread out on the snow.

My fleece jacket and pants turned into solid ice, my hands froze in my gloves. The next time I checked my phone, it was after midnight. Still seven more hours of darkness! I tried to focus like I would with a tough opponent, like I had with the big Russian. *You can do it, I thought. You can do anything, Rulon Gardner!*

That's what my mom and dad raised me to believe, that God hadn't put me in this world to fail. That's how I'd lived my life. When my teachers told me I wouldn't graduate high school, I just worked harder. During my junior year, one teacher said, "Rulon, you may graduate from high school, but forget about college." *Oh yeah?* I thought. *I'll show you.* It took me more than six years, but I got my degree from the University of Nebraska. Sports were the same way. I got to the Olympics on my own steam.

"I'm Rulon Gardner," I shouted at the snowy treetops. "I can do anything!" But my voice was swallowed in the wind.

Around 2:00 AM I heard the faint sound of a motor. Trent and Danny! My voice was too weak to holler, so I whistled as loud as I could. The sound came closer, then faded.

They missed me, I thought. *No one will find me now.* For the first time that night, for the first time in my life maybe, I was scared. I'd worked so hard to get strong, gold-medal strong. I'd tested that strength time and again, often foolishly. Now my strength wasn't enough. Nowhere near enough. I laid my head against the rough trunk of the tree and closed my eyes. *I can lick any opponent,* I thought, *but this? Lord, I am weak and you are strong. Infinitely strong. Help me.*

I drifted off. I dreamed that I was standing in a warm room with Jesus. Beside Him was my older brother Ronald. They were both smiling. I took a step toward them. "Wait, I don't want to be here," I said, "not yet." I woke with a start and struggled to my feet. Overhead the darkness was turning to gray. *How much longer until morning?* I shut my eyes to pray again. What came to me wasn't words, but the face of Jesus, like in my dream. In His expression, there was such infinite strength that I felt warmed. My eyes flew open. "I can do this," I said. With God anything is possible.

I stumbled back to the river and my sunken snowmobile. I was thirsty, so I bent down and put my lips to the rushing water. It was warmer than I expected, much warmer than the air, so I waded in. I let the water run through my frozen boots and lay back on a rock in the middle of the river, watching the stars melt into dawn. Was that the drone of an engine? I struggled up. An airplane was circling low overhead.

"Hey!" I croaked, waving my arms. The plane dropped something. A heavy coat landed on the snow. I got to my feet and started toward it. Then everything went black.

I awoke to a chopping sound. I was in a helicopter landing at a hospital in Idaho Falls. My core body temperature was eighty degrees, I heard the doctors say. They had to cut my boots off. I was shocked by the sight of my black, swollen feet. Eventually, I lost my middle toe. "You should have lost your feet," my doctor told me. "In fact, you should have died. The windchill was forty below. Normally, a person can't survive in those conditions. It's a good thing you're so strong."

All my life I've worked hard to get smarter, faster, stronger. But it wasn't bodily strength that got me through the long, freezing night in the mountains. It was Strength from the One who showed me that night what He had been telling me in the classroom, on the wrestling mat . . . all my life, really: You can do it. The only Strength that never fails.

STRENGTH FOR THE RACE

by Christine Conti

One day Guideposts sent me to interview marathon runner Bill Rodgers. At the end of the interview, I mentioned that I would be handing out water to runners in the next New York City Marathon.

"Great!" he said. "You have no idea how important water is to us runners."

Then he told me how, early in his racing career, he ran the first ten miles of a marathon without stopping for water. He was running well and he thought he didn't need it. At seventeen miles, however, his muscles cramped and he "hit the wall"; he had to stop.

"I now know," he explained, "that you have to keep replacing the water that you lose in sweat. And if you don't take any water early in the race, you'll dehydrate later on. The point is," Rodgers summed up, "you have to take water even when you think you don't need it."

What an obvious parallel between running a marathon and living the Christian life! How often I've felt so strong and confident that I didn't seem to need Jesus, yet Jesus said, "If any man thirst, let him come unto me, and drink" (John 7:37 KJV).

And Jesus might have added: "Even when you think you don't need it."

THE BREAKING OF THE BREAD

*by Mary Eva Smythe**
*Names have been changed.

The sweet aroma of Sally Lunn bread filled the kitchen as I lifted the loaf from the oven and set it on the bread rack. A giggle came from the other room, where our five-year-old grandson Bryan played with my husband. "Dinner in ten minutes, you two!" I called. "Wash up. We've got to hurry." Under my breath I added, "Before she gets here."

Whoever dreamed I could feel this way about Jane? We had had one of the best mother-in-law/daughter-in-law relationships in history, and I'd done my share of bragging about it. But all that ended the day before Thanksgiving, when our son Tom had stopped in as I was making a loaf of this very same bread.

"I'm sorry Jane can't join us tomorrow," I'd chatted, "but I understand she wants to see her own folks."

The tiredness in Tom's voice made me look up as he said, "It's more than that, Mom. Jane and I are splitting up."

His words floored me. I said, "Son, every marriage has its ups and downs. You expect them. You work through them."

"We've been trying to work through them for a long time. I didn't mention anything because I didn't want to worry you and Dad. We've tried and tried, but things change. Feelings change. Jane doesn't think more trying will help."

My mind went numb, unable to process the rest of what Tom was saying. This wasn't possible! Divorce happened to other families, not ours. Until now.

That was one of the most difficult holidays for our family. My initial shock had turned to mourning. No more happy family holidays or vacations. No more united fronts at Bryan's Little League games. And poor Tom looked so miserable I wanted to cry.

Yes, feelings change, and of course I didn't know the inner workings of Tom's marriage, but how could Jane call it quits? Couldn't she think of Tom's feelings? Of Bryan's needs? Of a family torn apart?

How can she do this to us?

As the days passed, I began to feel more and more resentful. Once, I enumerated Jane's charms; now, I found myself agreeing with a friend who was berating her: "Any mother worth her salt would think of her child rather than her own selfish whims."

Finally, I vowed to cut all ties with this daughter-in-law. If she wanted out of our family, out is what she would get.

Now and then guilt got the better of me and I went to God in prayer. I prayed for our son in his misery and for little Bryan, but I could not bring myself to include Jane in my prayers. After all, we'd welcomed Jane into our family, only to be betrayed.

One day during a particularly degrading diatribe of mine, my husband broke his silence. "Don't you think you're going overboard with your bitterness?" Ed asked. "We've got to think of Bryan."

I had thought of Bryan. In fact, we'd seen far more of him than ever before, and for that I was thankful. Now that Tom lived across town, it often wasn't possible for him to keep Bryan when Jane had late afternoon appointments to show real estate. Ed and I were delighted to help.

But when Jane dropped off and picked up Bryan, I spoke to her as little as possible. I was careful that we finished supper before pickup time and had Bryan's things by the door so there'd be no need for Jane to tarry. Often I sent Bryan out to meet her as her car pulled up.

Today we were right on schedule. I gave a final stir to the stew and called Ed and Bryan.

But just as I carted the steaming pot to the table, there came a knock on the door. And there stood Jane, a half hour early. If that wasn't bad enough, I heard my husband ask her to join us for dinner.

As she stooped to kiss Bryan's cheek, awkwardness filled each nook and cranny of the kitchen.

"Come," I said in a strained voice. "I'll set another place."

"I—" Jane glanced at the table. Her face brightened.

"Oh, Mother Smythe," she said, using the name she'd chosen for me. "Could I? You've made Sally Lunn bread. I could smell it the minute Dad opened the door."

Bryan happily showed off the bread he'd helped make. Then the four of us sat down to eat.

At first our conversation was stilted, centering on Bryan and his kindergarten activities, but gradually the silences grew less strained. Near the end of the meal, I looked at Jane and found her looking at me.

Then a strange thing happened. At the same moment we both picked up our bread and broke it.

A feeling I cannot describe came over me. It was as if the bread in my hand possessed an unseen power. The words "I am the Bread of Life" echoed in my head, each time softer and more soothing than before. I remembered how often Jesus had broken bread with His followers and prayed we'd all be one, known by our love rather than our grudges.

More times than I could count, I had held the bread at Communion, the ultimate reminder that Jesus had come not to condemn but to forgive. Yet for months I had been condemning my daughter-in-law. Not once had I thought of the pain she must be feeling in this separation. I told myself I'd been thinking only of my son and grandson, but in fact, I had been nursing my own sense of betrayal and bitterness. We at this table had broken bread together. I knew that I needed to make my humble confession to God.

With a feeling of unworthiness, I held the bread in my hand and silently asked for the Lord's pardon for my offenses. And amazingly, gradually, I found my tension ebbing away.

The aroma of the bread blended with Bryan's chatter and we lingered at the table after the meal was over.

As Jane and Bryan prepared to leave, I hugged Bryan and then turned toward Jane. My need to be forgiven lay in my throat in a liquid lump. Suddenly she flung her arms around me and we held each other.

"I'm sorry, Mother Smythe," she said. "Very sorry."

Then she turned to Ed. "Dad—" her voice broke. With a quick hug for him she was out the door with Bryan.

I can't say the divorce proceedings that followed were easy for any of us, but I can say that relinquishing resentment opened the way for healing. My attempt at placing blame had not lessened the heartache; it had added more hurt.

Granted, I still regret that our son's marriage didn't survive, but recent Thanksgiving celebrations have found me grateful for other things. I am thankful Ed and I are close to our grandson and that Jane and I can talk with the warmth of friends. And I recall those disciples on the road to Emmaus, who didn't recognize the stranger who joined them until Jesus was made "known to them in the breaking of the bread." Most of all, I'm thankful He still makes His healing presence known to His disciples today.

KNEELING AT THE FOOT OF THE CROSS

by Julia Attaway

I hadn't talked to my friend Geoffrey in quite awhile, although there was no particular reason for our lack of conversation. Knowing that he was in the middle of an increasingly messy custody dispute, one Sunday after church I finally made it my business to track him down.

"How are you?" I asked. Over the years we'd talked a lot about prayer, so Geoffrey knew I was asking about both his emotional and spiritual state.

"Actually," he said, "I'm doing quite well. It's been really hard these past few months, but my prayer life is amazingly strong. I sort of stumbled onto a technique that has helped me enormously."

I asked him what it was.

"Well, whenever I find myself getting angry or bitter, I bring myself to the foot of the Cross and kneel there. And then I mentally bring my former wife to kneel at my side."

"Wow," I said, "that sounds really hard."

"It can be," he replied. "Sometimes it takes a long time to let go enough to bring her there. But the way I look at it, if I can't kneel with someone in front of Jesus, my problems are much bigger than the problems I face in this world. So whenever I recognize an obstacle in my heart to that kind of union, I just pick it up and hang it on that Cross."

It takes courage to use Geoffrey's technique, as I discover every time I try it. It's the kind of courage I need more of.

*If we in our own strength confide,
our striving would be losing.*
—MARTIN LUTHER

THE COLORS OF LIFE

by Raul Ruiz

Life was bursting with color in the small sheepshearing community of
Eola, Texas, where I grew up. The blue sky stretching far and wide.
The green pasture grass waving in the breeze. The leathery brown faces of
the men who sheared off white clumps of wool from the sheep. My imagination was seized by those colors and as a young boy I wore my crayons
down to stubs trying to capture their beauty on paper. When I got a drawing just right, I felt an incredible closeness to God, as if I were being
granted a fleeting glimpse of His creation.

I joined my father and brothers in the sheepshearing business. I learned
how to hold a sheep steady while I removed its delicate belly wool, how to
keep from nicking even the most unruly animal. Sometimes, we'd go out to
neighboring ranches with other shearers for work, camping out overnight.
I'd watch the light from the fire play across the faces of the older shearers as
they strummed their guitars and sang. Their faces filled my sketchbooks. I
respected—even admired—them, but I was always the observer.

I continued to sketch from photos and on location. Eventually, I went
and bought paints and brushes. At last, I could really capture God's palette.

"This one's real good, Raul," said my brother Rudy, who loved my
painting of a Rambouillet sheep with its arching double horns. "Yeah,
brother," added my brother Danny. "It's almost as good as the one you

did of Papa and us shearing the sheep. You're a real artist." Deep inside, I knew art was what I was meant to do, but I didn't see how I could ever hope to be anything but a sheepshearer.

Then one day in the summer of 1987 the owner of the ranch where we were working noticed me perched on a fence, sketching. "What's your son doing over there?" he asked my father as he headed toward me. He studied the drawing in my hands, then picked up one of a horse peering over a weathered wooden fence. "How much do you want for this one?" he asked.

I didn't know what to say. All I could think was *Someone wants to buy my drawings!*

"Well, do you want to sell your work?" the owner asked me.

"The lot goes for thirty-five dollars," I said boldly. He took out his wallet and counted thirty-five dollars into my hand. Just like that, I'd sold my early sketches and drawings.

Some time later, a lady from another ranch came over and bought one hundred dollars worth of sketches. Other ranchers visited and asked me to do paintings of prize sheep. I went from ranch to ranch, sketching and painting sheep, horses, cowboys, saddles, shearers, anything people wanted. It was like someone had suddenly flicked a switch and shone a light on my gift. By 1989, my work was selling well enough for me to open a studio in San Angelo, Texas, about twenty-four miles from Eola. I spent long, sunny days at my easel, the smell of my paints mingling with the scent of wild-flowers. I was what I always wanted to be—a successful artist. I met my wife Norma and soon the Lord blessed us with two daughters, Erica and Andrea.

Then a strange thing happened: As I struggled to meet the growing demands of my business, the colors I painted gradually stopped looking as vibrant to me. Sometimes I felt so detached from my work it was like I was painting by numbers. Little by little I found myself withdrawing—from my wife and daughters, from my passion for my work, from my identity as a painter.

Depression set in. Someday people are going to find out I don't feel it anymore. I'm not the artist they think I am.

I couldn't tell my family what was wrong because I was afraid of disappointing them. I lost weight and became extremely fatigued. I had unexplained aches and pains. My wife took me to doctor after doctor. None of them could figure out what was wrong with me.

By 1995, my business was in real trouble. I hardly painted anymore and my studio was in disarray. One day, when a customer came, I fled into the back room, leaving my wife to handle him. *How can I sell my paintings when I don't feel like the painter who did them?* I was struggling. My gift was gone. I sank onto a mess of dried-out paint jars, unused brushes and canvas, burying my head in my lap. Norma came in and sat beside me. "Just keep on going," she said, gently. "You haven't failed. I sold the one with the sheep grazing at sunset."

"It doesn't make any difference," I said. "We're going to have to close the studio." It didn't even bother me. I'd lost all interest in what was once my dream.

A few weeks later, I shut down the studio and sold the last few pictures in our closet. I took a part-time job in a frame shop, though the physical pains I suffered were so bad I wondered how I would make it through each day.

One afternoon I got a visit from Rudy and Danny. They made no mention of my troubles; we just talked and somehow they got me to laugh again. I thought back to growing up with them and all those times I'd hunt around for scraps of paper to draw on or stay up late and sketch under the stars.

Before they left, they hugged me. "We love you, brother," Rudy said. Their visit gave me such a boost that after they went on their way, I did some painting. A while later the phone rang. I could barely recognize the voice of my brother Rufus. "Danny and Rudy have been in a car accident,

Raul," he said. "It was real bad . . . they're dead." But they were just here. Their laughter was still ringing in my ears.

That's when the light in my life went out entirely. The physical pain I had been suffering was nothing compared to the inner anguish over their deaths. I wouldn't answer letters or phone calls. When I sat at my window and looked out over the Texas landscape, all the colors had turned to shades of gray, like on an old TV set. The bluebonnets in the fields, the plump white clouds—all of it had faded. *Will I never paint again?*

Norma kept inviting family and friends over to visit, but love too had slipped into the gray area. One afternoon, my brother-in-law came over for lunch. "How are you doing?" he asked.

"The same," I said.

He leaned over the table, looked at me intently and said, "Listen, Raul, the only thing that will get you through this is faith in God. The only thing."

But how could I feel close to God now? I'd always felt closest to Him when painting His creation, but I couldn't see its beauty anymore. It was as if my spiritual lifeline—my art—had been cut.

After Alex left I opened up my Bible, more out of desperation than hope. I forced myself to read words I hadn't looked at in a long time. Day after day I'd read, even if I didn't understand. I willed my eyes across the verses, Old Testament and New, no matter how bad I felt. The physical act of reading became my weapon against the doubts and fears that had darkened my world. I forced myself to read and reread until the words became so vivid they were like colors. I got down on my knees and prayed every morning, focusing on the image of Jesus Christ until He became real to me and I loved Him.

On the morning of August 6, 1995, I was praying as usual. *Lord, I believe now that only You can help me be well again. Only You.* All at once an incredible sense of release spread through me, a sort of inner heat and light. I touched my chest, my head, my stomach. My pain was gone! I jumped to my feet, amazed at how I felt. No pain!

Ravenous, I ran to the kitchen. I threw open the refrigerator and caught my breath. There I saw a kind of miracle. The soft-white eggs, the red-hot peppers, the emerald-green cucumbers, the canary-yellow lemons. I wanted to eat them all, take in those brilliant colors and feel them coursing through me. I started chopping onions and peppers, cracking eggs, pouring orange juice. I made myself a good breakfast and took it into the living room. And there before me was a picture of a cowboy painting I'd done, awash in vivid greens and blues and browns. *Thank You, Lord, for showing me such wonder again.*

When my wife came home that evening, I exclaimed. "Norma, Jesus healed me today. Things will be different now."

And they were. I asked forgiveness from my wife and daughters for being so distant and we slowly became a family again. Then, when I was absolutely sure it was what the Lord wanted, I began to paint. But it was different this time. I had made God my sole strength and His love flowed through my brush every time I drew it across the canvas. I held tight to the promise in Proverbs 16:3 (NIV): "Commit to the Lord whatever you do, and your plans will succeed."

All my life I'd painted the colors I saw around me, but now I'd found an endless palette of colors inside me, ones I saw only when I reached out to the Creator. I was in the dark a long time. Then faith in Jesus lit me up inside and showed me all the colors of life.

IT WILL BE ALL RIGHT

by Frances O. Jansen

The excruciating pain in my back had been getting worse for months. Diathermy treatments, massage, bed rest and painkillers had barely eased my distress.

Surgery terrified me. I tried to fall back on my faith in God and kept repeating the platitudes I had heard all my life: "Have faith—God never puts burdens on you heavier than you can bear." Nothing helped.

My husband felt helpless. I was a member of a Protestant church. He was a "fallen-away" who had not prayed since he was a boy. On one of the days when I was having an especially difficult time, Elmer asked me, "Where's that Supreme Being you're always praying to? Why doesn't He help you now?"

All I could do was answer weakly, "There's a reason for this."

That night I sank into despair. Silently I cried out to the Lord, demanding to know, *Why me, God? What is this plague You have sent me?*

About midnight, sleep took over. What happened next I could not share with anyone, not even my husband, lest people think I had gone over the edge.

I slept facing the hallway, where a small light burned during the night. The bedroom door was open. Suddenly I opened my eyes, and there in the doorway—for just a second or two—stood Jesus, His right hand outstretched. And just before He disappeared from view, He said, "It will be all right." His white robe seemed to leave a bright glow for another brief instant.

I glanced at the clock on the dresser. The lighted dial read 2:43 AM. I turned my head toward my husband and heard only his gentle snore.

An indescribable peace entered my body. The pain was still there, but somehow it didn't matter. Taking my cane, I made my way into the hallway, half expecting to see Jesus still there.

The words echoed in my head: *It will be all right.* I had not been dreaming. I went into the bathroom and stared into the mirror. There was a strange look in my eyes, a stare of awe, of amazement, of delight. I felt wonderful!

The next day I found out why Jesus had come. The day began like most. I eased my aching body out of bed. Yet I felt so confident that I decided to get dressed. As I put my left leg into my girdle, I screamed in agony, and Elmer came running.

An ambulance took me to the hospital. Tests showed a herniated disk in the lower back. My doctor and several experts agreed that I could heal without surgery. I spent thirty days in traction.

Each day as I awoke I heard in my mind: *It will be all right.* It was. On the thirty-first day I was able to get out of bed. The next day I went home and into a rented hospital bed, then to a wheelchair, crutches, and finally a cane. I wore a back-support girdle and a back brace. I still wear the girdle daily, and occasionally I have to use the back brace.

During the following years several tragedies touched my life. "How can you be so strong?" a friend asked. It would have been a perfect time to tell her that Jesus had appeared to me, sent by God to give me the assurance that has carried me through misfortune and good times alike. But I held back for fear of what she and others might think.

It's been more than twenty years since Jesus appeared to me. Recently in church a soloist sang the hymn "Blessed Assurance, Jesus Is Mine!" and I felt my message from God should no longer be a secret.

I have never questioned why God sent His Son to visit me that night. I truly believe I would not have been able to carry the burden without the optimistic attitude He furnished me. By telling me, "It will be all right," Jesus helped me bear the load.

THE BUBBLE

by Marion Bond West

I stood in the telephone booth at St. Mary's Hospital in Athens, Georgia, and dialed my daughter Julie's number. I never expected to be afraid like this again. Gene, my husband of nearly four years, had been hospitalized and was to have angioplasty (surgery on his blood vessels). My mind knew that he was going to be fine, but my emotions refused to be sensible, instead reaching back nearly eight years and feeling the anguish of the time when Jerry, my then-husband, was dying of a brain tumor.

"I can't do it, Julie. I can't go up in that room. I'm afraid of the elevator, the ambulances, the nurses' smiles, the forms, the IVs. And I'm angry that I should have a husband in the hospital again. I can't do this again! Do you hear?" I was crying, shaking, and I wanted to hit something—anything.

Julie let me wind down. Then, calmly, she said, "Mother, you know what you've done? You've gotten outside The Bubble. Just get back into The Bubble, get on the elevator, and go to Gene. You are fine. You can do this—in The Bubble."

I stood there blankly for a moment, then I remembered. The Bubble is Jesus. It's a formula the children and I came up with when their father was dying. If you get "in Jesus" (see Ephesians 1:3), you can almost "float" through any situation, and He takes all stress while you "hide," protected in Him.

I emerged from the telephone booth back inside The Bubble. I punched the "Up" button at the elevator. I wasn't alone or vulnerable. I was fine and Gene was too.

The Lord stood at my side and gave me strength. . . .
—2 TIMOTHY 4:17 (NIV)

DANCING WITH JESUS

by Evelyn Bence

Where I grew up, dancing was as forbidden as stealing. But if I seriously thought about this prohibition, it was okay with me. It saved me from what I felt would surely be my fateful embarrassment: not being asked onto the floor. It always hung over me, this dread of being unchosen—like the last person selected for a softball team.

So there was reason for my surprise at what played through my mind one morning when I, as instructed, meditated on Jesus. At a breakfast meeting for lay ministers, I listened as the leader read the first half of John 4, the story of Jesus' conversation with the woman at the well. The leader gave us questions to consider, most of which prodded us to think about the personal nature of Jesus' encounter—such a long and loving conversation with a Samaritan, a stranger, a woman, a sinner.

Before we all left that breakfast to face our days filled with work, we were asked to sit and listen to—relax and enjoy—a piece of music, unfamiliar to me. Never having heard it, I couldn't anticipate the words, the melody, the flow; I simply closed my eyes and concentrated on Jesus, talking to me as attentively as He had the Samaritan. But the music seemed to take over.

On the screen of my eyelid, Jesus and I started to dance, not like lovers—although we two were alone on the floor and He had chosen me as His partner—but like children, freely, joyously, circling each other, touching hands, laughing with our eyes and hearts, celebrating life.

For five or ten minutes or an hour, maybe, I was lost in the reverie of movement inspired by sound. I wished and wished it could go on forever.

The music didn't end abruptly, but it gradually lost its power and momentum. While the last low, slow notes played, it seemed Jesus held my gaze and backed away from me, toward the glassed door to the outside world.

My eyes, I knew, reflected my disappointment, my desire for the music and dance to continue. Still walking backward He spoke to me, though they were words I didn't particularly want to hear. "Life is a war," He said, "not a dance."

"No, don't say it," I replied silently.

But He was as intent on speaking as the music was on ending. "We can and will dance whenever we have a battle victory to celebrate. But now, you have to go back to your post and watch, even fight."

In the scenario of my mind, I reached out my hand to urge Him not to go, and He kept talking, though now in whispers. "I'll not leave you, I promise, ever, even in the midst of the battles. You won't always feel My presence this close, but I'll be right behind you. Remember, when we win, we can dance again, and someday the music will never stop."

Obviously the promise of never-ending music was for some future day, because the next moment was filled with silence, the record having circled until the needle hit a band. I opened my eyes, sad to be reminded that I was sitting on a folding chair and that the expanse of hard wood floor that separated me from the record player was bare and had been all along.

I don't know what the other people in the room imagined during those reflective minutes. Shortly we all left, each to her own battlefield. But I, for one, walked out ready to tackle any Goliath.

I'd been chosen—the fact filled me with confidence. But my new courage went deeper than that. I left the meeting a little less burdened by unrealistic expectations. Here and now in this world, the song always will end, even after we've been asked to waltz. But now I see that that has nothing to do with being abandoned to standing—or fighting—alone.

The music is going to start up again. And every time it does, the dance is going to be a taste of heaven, where the joy of love is never going to lose its power.

· PART 10 ·

Glimpses of Jesus in One Another

IN SOME MYSTICAL WAY, we can be as Christ to each other. This is especially true within the Christian community. The apostle Paul told the church at Corinth: "Now you are the body of Christ, and each one of you is a part of it" (1 Corinthians 12:27 NIV).

Jesus indicates that He also is present in the stranger. He describes a Judgment Day, when people will stand before Him and ask, "Lord, when did we see you hungry or thirsty or a stranger or needing clothes . . . ?" His answer? "Whatever you did not do for one of the least of these, you did not do for me" (Matthew 25:44–45 NIV). Jesus is the recipient of our kind—as well as our disrespectful—acts to our fellow human beings.

The short pieces in this section give momentary glimpses of Jesus as seen in the lives and service of God's people. The longer stories give an insightful view of Christ at work in His world, through human acts of mercy, words of love, eyes of faith.

With hymnwriter Charles Scott, join me in praying that Jesus this day and always will continue to

> Open my eyes, that I may see
> Glimpses of truth thou hast for me.

THE FACES OF HOPE

by John DeVito

It was 7:40 AM that sparkling September day when I unlocked our office on the eighty-seventh floor of Tower One in the World Trade Center. Though it meant getting up at five o'clock in my home about forty miles north in suburban Westchester County, I loved these quiet moments before the frenzy of another day's trading began.

Alone in the office, I could listen to the voice of the great building itself. Ironworkers will tell you that steel sings; to me, whose parents came here from Italy, the sighing of the mighty steel girders was the notes of an opera.

Sure, this Wall Street area, where I'd worked more than half my forty-five years, was a competitive, me-first kind of place. But standing there at the window with a large coffee from my favorite place on Fulton Street, I liked to spend a few moments taking in the beauty. The Statue of Liberty . . . the Hudson River glinting in the sunlight. This was my town. From here I could look down on the rooftops of Brooklyn, where I'd grown up and where my parents still lived. Even when it came time for college I hadn't wanted to go anywhere else—I got my degrees a couple of miles uptown at New York University.

My team at May Davis was starting to arrive. We were a small investment banking firm, raising capital for start-up companies. "Morning, Harry," I greeted my friend and our head trader, Harry Ramos. "Morning,

Adam, Hong, Dominique, Jason." Fourteen of us in all, ten men, four women. As the hum of a busy office picked up, I checked my e-mail, glanced through the papers on my desk, reached for the phone to—

The room lurched right. I nearly fell off my chair, then clutched the desk as the room jolted left. An earthquake? A ceiling tile clattered onto my desk. Light fixtures dangled, wires spitting. "It's a bomb!" someone yelled.

For a stunned moment we stared at one another. "I'll go check!" I ran into the corridor. Smoke. People peering from office doorways. I groped my way through the haze, past the elevators, down the hall to . . . I stopped.

The rest of the corridor was gone. Where a row of doors had been, I found myself staring down into a hellhole of fire and twisted steel.

Burning debris cascaded around me. Without thinking, I snatched a broken piece of wallboard and beat at the flames. It was a moment before sanity returned. I rushed back to my office, where others were doing futile things too: collecting files, packing up big desktop computers. Outside the window where I'd stood sipping coffee, things were falling. Papers, hunks of metal.

Dust and smoke seeped from the ceiling. As chief operating officer I knew I should give some kind of direction, but what? Where to turn? I was a churchgoing man, but at that moment of fear and mounting chaos God seemed awfully far away. Was my duty to stay and safeguard company property? Strange how slow the mind is to grasp enormity . . .

Adam Mayblum had kept his head and was ripping up his shirt, passing out strips to use as face masks. At last reality got through to me: *Get your people out of this building.* I ran to my desk and called my wife Marilyn. "I love you, Mar! Tell the girls I love them!"

I grabbed a half-gallon bottle of water, got people to moisten their makeshift masks. Some of the staff still looked undecided. "Joanne! Sam! Everybody! Let's go! Leave everything!"

In the corridor the smoke had grown thicker. "Not the elevators!" I

shouted. Pressing the wet cloth over my nose, I led the way . . . right . . .
then left . . . Where was the exit sign? I'd passed it a thousand times,
scarcely seeing it—who takes stairs from the eighty-seventh floor? We
were almost at the chasm where the hallway ended when I saw the sign
glowing redly through the gloom. If the floor had fallen in a few yards
nearer, there would have been no exit.

The stairwell was filled with acrid smoke and fleeing people. Narrow
. . . stay together . . . go single file. "Put your hand on my shoulder," I told
Jason. "Everyone hold onto the one in front." The fourteen of us formed
a chain and started down. Eighty-sixth floor . . . eighty-fifth . . . Around
us people were saying an airplane had struck the tower. It was incompre-
hensible. Yet there we were, struggling through the smoke, the ordinari-
ness of the day torn asunder.

At the seventy-eighth floor the stairway suddenly ended. Seventy-
eight was a transfer floor. The stairway continued somewhere on the
other side of an open area around the elevator banks. We stepped into a
scene of pandemonium. In the choking dust hundreds of people milled,
looking for an exit. From the ceiling exposed wires sent showers of sparks
into the crowd. Small fires crept along the floor. There were screams, people crying, people praying.

In the press and the confusion, our human chain broke up. By the
time we located the stairs I'd lost track of Harry, Hong and several others.
"Go ahead!" I told the rest, "I'll stay and look for them."

Jason pulled my arm. "John! Don't be foolish. This building's on fire!
Think of Marilyn, your girls!"

Maybe the others were ahead of us, maybe they'd found another staircase. We went on. Seventy-third . . . seventy-second. More and more people with every floor, progress so slow. As a terribly burned woman was
carried past, I battled the fear clawing inside me. I wondered where God
was in all this terror.

After thirty floors my legs were shaking with fatigue. I stopped, passed around the half-gallon bottle. Fifty-fourth . . . fifty-third . . . Almost half an hour and we'd only come this far!

Still fifty floors to go. A stream of water from the automatic sprinklers was making the steps slippery. People stumbled and fell. Others helped them up. I could no longer see anyone from my office. Forty-sixth . . . forty-third . . . forty-first . . .

It was then that I saw him. He was a fireman toiling up the stairs, heavy equipment strapped to his back and sweat streaming down his face. He stopped just below me and tugged off his helmet. Short-cropped blond hair, brilliant blue eyes, the map of Ireland on his face. He was red with exertion—but there was a glow about him I thought was more than that. Why did I feel I ought to know him?

"You look like you need some water," I said, holding out the half-full bottle.

The blue eyes looked into mine. "I'm all right," he told me. "Give it to somebody else."

He put his helmet back on and kept climbing. I went on down. Thirty-eighth floor . . . thirty-sixth. Give it to somebody else. And suddenly I knew whose face I'd seen above that fireman's raincoat.

It was the face of Jesus.

Thirty-fifth floor . . . thirty-fourth. I began to notice something I'd seen without taking it in. In that stairwell jammed with terrified people, there'd been no shoving. Wedged together in a narrow stairway of a burning building, no one pushed ahead of the slow movers. Over and over I'd witnessed just the opposite. The handicapped given precedence. Men stepping aside for women. The young giving place to the gray-haired. As injured and burn victims were carried past, everyone flattened against the wall, called encouragement, waited. Same too as the firefighters climbed up.

Twenty-ninth floor . . . twenty-eighth. I blinked. That young Asian woman with her arm around a frail older lady—surely it was Jesus who looked out of her eyes! Again . . . I glimpsed Him in the eyes of the Pakistani man motioning me to go first. God far away? God was right here, all around me on that crowded stairway, wherever one person reached out to help another.

Once more the water bottle came back to me. All those hot, hurrying people, but each one took only a sip or a drop to wet a handkerchief. Give it to somebody else. All around me the face of Jesus. In the caring, generous, giving people of a competitive, me-first world.

Three exhausted firemen were on the landing of the fourteenth floor. I left the bottle with them. Tenth floor. Seventh. And suddenly I was outside.

My relief was chilled by the scream of sirens. Fire trucks everywhere. Ambulances. Police shouting, "Move! Keep moving! Don't look up!"

And at that, of course, everyone looked up. A giant plume of black smoke trailed from high in the building. No . . . from both buildings! Our twin tower, Tower Two, also on fire? Around me people were saying two airplanes had hit. Two? But that had to mean . . .

Someone shouted my name; next instant I was embracing three of my team! "Get out of here!" a policeman yelled at us. I looked up.

And saw the impossible. Tower Two was falling. The whole enormous structure thundering down.

A deafening roar, people shrieking. I ran, but the hot black cloud came faster. In seconds I was smothered in a stinking, suffocating blanket of heat and dust. Blinded, stumbling, I could only pray I was running in a straight line and not back toward the collapsing giant. Around me were cries, running feet, but I could see no one. It was darkness as I'd never imagined the dark. An organic, breathing, malevolent blackness.

And suddenly I knew what this dark cloud was. Minutes earlier I'd looked into the face of Jesus. Now I was encountering the darkness of evil.

If Jesus was love, this was hate. Tripping, choking, gasping, knowing now that this destruction was deliberate, I understood that this is what hate always does. Blinds us to one another, spreads its all-obscuring cloud to keep us from seeing one anothers' faces.

Through squinted eyes, I saw light ahead. The putrid, strangling cloud was thinner. I burst into a store—a record shop—and gulped the sweet cold air. Someone gave me water, urged me to sit, but after calling Marilyn and my parents, I had to keep walking. Heading north . . . anywhere away from that faceless night. Chinatown. The Village. Washington Square Park. Looking at people. Looking at Jesus.

And looking for a church. Any church, where I could tell Him that my life would be forever different. I had always believed in Him; now I'd seen Him.

I caught sight of myself too, reflected in a store window, and understood why some people drew back as I approached. I was blanketed in ash, a gray specter. Others, though, ran toward me. Reached out, grasped my hand, hugged me.

Somehow I'd come clear to the NYU campus. I went into a church and knelt in a pew. And for the first time, I cried.

Marilyn had told me not to battle the crowds trying to get out of the city; her cousins on Leroy Street were expecting me. I walked there from the church. The Perazzo family rushed down the steps of the brownstone to greet me, let me shower, tried to get me to lie down. But I couldn't stay indoors, couldn't handle walls, a ceiling. All afternoon I sat outside on the stoop, under that bright blue sky, my back to the smoke shrouding the south of my city.

When I learned that Tower One had fallen too, faces sprang in front of me. The blue-eyed fireman who wanted me to give the water to somebody else. The policeman standing at his post calling out to others to move away.

And the face of Harry Ramos. Phone calls had located all the rest of our staff. Only later did we learn that trim, athletic Harry had stayed behind on the thirty-sixth floor to help a heavyset stranger who could walk no farther.

Bobby Perazzo couldn't resist telling his neighbors on Leroy Street, "My cousin was there! He was in Tower One!"

The word spread among passersby. A tourist couple from Utah embraced me. A Puerto Rican lady said, "Vaya con Dios," It was Jesus, of course. All of them. In a burning building. On a New York street. Whenever darkness threatens to overwhelm us. Wherever love glows on a human face.

*You show that you are a letter from Christ . . .
written not with ink but with the Spirit
of the living God, not on tablets of stone
but on tablets of human hearts.*

—2 CORINTHIANS 3:3 (NIV)

I HAD TO WRITE BACK

by David Griesel

The sun was high in the sky that afternoon last September when I drove out to check the cattle on our family farm. I looked out over the fields. Something glittered in the distance near a gnarled cedar tree. Curious, I drove over. Snagged in the tree's branches was a deflated balloon. I pulled it down carefully and found a note attached. "Dear Caroline," it said. "We love you and miss you very much. Love, your big sisters, Brittany and Victoria."

On the back of the note their mother wrote: "If you get this, the girls would like a sign that you're in heaven with Jesus and that you know we love you." Then I saw the return address. The wind had carried this balloon clear across Texas to me in Oklahoma.

The next day at work I showed the note to my assistant. Together we composed a response: "Dear Brittany and Victoria, I was so excited to get the balloon you sent to heaven. Jesus and I are having lots of fun. I know that one day we'll be together again. God's Blessings, Jesus and Caroline."

We put our note in the mail along with a separate message for the parents, explaining who we were. I hoped it would help, but we'd never know for sure.

A week later I opened my mailbox and found a letter from Texas. "Thank you so much," Caroline's mother wrote. "God truly sent an unmistakable sign of His love through you."

I had my answer.

JOIN THE FAMILY

by Melody Bonnette

I returned home from church on Christmas Eve, my spirit revived and refreshed. I pulled up a chair next to the fireplace and opened my favorite Christmas novel, Marjorie Holmes's *Two from Galilee*, the story of Joseph and Mary, a couple searching for shelter on a cold winter night.

My eighteen-year-old son Christopher sat down beside me. "Mom, can Jeff spend Christmas with us?" My son's friend Jeff had been staying with us for the past few months. I had assumed that he would be spending Christmas with his own family.

"Does he have to, Christopher?" I asked. Lately our house had been so full of our children's friends that I had hoped to have just our family together on Christmas morning.

"Mom, he doesn't really have anywhere else to go."

"Okay," I said. "That's fine." I smiled weakly.

I looked down at the novel resting on my lap and remembered the minister's words I'd heard just an hour earlier: "When we serve others, we honor Jesus within them, just as an unknowing innkeeper did when he found room in his stable for Joseph and Mary."

I quickly called out to my son, who was on his way upstairs. "Christopher, it's really okay. I'd like to celebrate Christmas with Jeff." Actually, it wasn't just okay, it was a wonderful idea! Why, I had just been given the opportunity to open my home to a young man who, like Joseph and Mary, needed a warm and safe place to stay on Christmas Eve.

The next morning when Jeff came downstairs, I reached out and hugged him. "Merry Christmas, Jeff," I said. "Come join the family."

NOT IN MY NEIGHBORHOOD

by Ed Huber

No one can escape problems and crises in life—they are the shadows that contrast with the sunshine of good times. I've had my share of sunshine and shadows. But one of the most serious crises I ever faced involved the restaurant I own in downtown Manhattan.

Delmonico's is on Beaver Street, a narrow winding thoroughfare in the financial district. The name Delmonico's is, I'm proud to say, a distinguished one, dating back to 1827 when two Swiss immigrants, the Del-Monico brothers—Giovanni and Pietro—opened the doors of a restaurant that would gain worldwide fame. Charles Dickens and Mark Twain dined there, as did Jenny Lind, Lillian Russell, Diamond Jim Brady and every President from James Monroe to Franklin D. Roosevelt. In time, the restaurant closed, but the name continued.

My dad, an Austrian immigrant, came to America in 1929 and began as a dishwasher at a humble establishment. He worked his way up to chef and eventually bought out the restaurant owner.

Dad warned me about following in his footsteps. "Don't come into a business where you have to work fifteen hours a day," he said. But I thrived on it. I earned a degree in hotel management and joined the family enterprise. By the 1970s I owned several restaurants.

One day in 1981 a friend told me about a property at 56 Beaver Street. When I saw the shuttered brownstone I said, "Why, this is the old Delmonico's!"

I made up my mind on the spot to reopen the historic establishment. I leased the building and at great expense restored the Victorian dining room, with its leaded windows, crystal chandeliers and dark paneling. Then we gutted the basement, installed gracefully curved steps and added another whole dining room, similar to the one upstairs. Wall Street brokers and blue-chip CEOs soon took to the "new" Delmonico's.

But in spring 1988, word came that the city was planning to open a shelter for the homeless just three doors away. In shock, I had visions of derelicts and bag ladies lined up outside, panhandling our customers. I knew the bad effect that could have. What if our customers stopped coming in? How would I repay my loans or keep my staff? I could see my investment and seven years of hard work sliding away.

It wasn't that I didn't feel for the homeless and hungry who would be coming to the shelter. I knew that the problem of these needy people affects all of us. Like many others, I had made stabs at helping: I'd brought bags of good used clothes from my wife Mary to one of my kitchen workers. I even helped at the inner-city soup kitchen run by our church, St. Elizabeth's, in Wyckoff, New Jersey. And like others, I'd pressed money into trembling outstretched hands. No, I was not unaware of the homeless, or uncaring. But the very existence of my restaurant was at stake.

That night I told Mary how the whole Beaver Street neighborhood was up in arms. We were going to sue, to block the shelter from coming in.

To my chagrin, Mary wasn't all that sympathetic. "These are human beings, Ed," she reminded me. "I'm not at all sure you're being Christian about this."

"Mary," I said impatiently, "you're not here to judge the situation. This could ruin us." I reminded her of what had happened to the restaurants on

28th Street when the city opened welfare hotels nearby. They went broke. "Being 'Christian' has nothing to do with it," I said. "This is business!"

My wife was well-meaning but naive. I remembered a day seven years earlier, when I showed her Delmonico's for the first time. It was bitter cold, and as we came out of the Battery Park garage, we passed a bag lady huddled in a cardboard box. Mary insisted we go back to help her. "She's there every day," I said. "Maybe she likes living that way."

"Ed," Mary replied, "nobody likes freezing in a box."

In the weeks after I learned about the shelter, a sizable contingent of us—residents, restaurateurs and business leaders in the Wall Street area—held a series of strategy meetings, many of them at Delmonico's. I spoke up firmly at those meetings. We formed the Coalition to Advance Lower Manhattan (CALM) and got up a $50,000 war chest. We held press conferences, we demonstrated. The area was too congested already, we insisted; there were other sites. But after a stormy hearing, the local community board voted to go ahead with the project.

CALM countered by filing our lawsuit. We felt we had good grounds. For one thing, the shelter site flooded every time it rained. Why would they put homeless people down there? Furthermore, there was no access for the handicapped.

At home, it bothered me that Mary remained unsympathetic. "Being a Christian means taking risks," she'd say. "Seems to me you're not willing to take any. You're not going to win anyway."

My wife was right about one thing: You can't fight City Hall. The city put pumps in that damp basement and complied with all the building codes.

Our lawyer advised us to settle out of court. He also reminded us that Trinity Church, the historic Wall Street church, was going to run the shelter for the city. Now, if we did have to back down, at least I had some hope: I felt the church could run the shelter better than the city. These were Christian people. And I was a Christian. Maybe they would listen to our grievances.

Reluctantly we agreed to withdraw our suit.

"We lost our case," I glumly told Mary. "But at least Trinity Church is in on it now," I added lamely.

"I'm sorry, honey," she said, patting my arm. "But you know, it's not too late to change your thinking—reverse the negatives and make them positive."

In October, Canon Lloyd Casson, Trinity's rector, brought both sides together, and out of that the city, at the behest of the church, met many of CALM's conditions—the most important being the creation of an advisory board made up of residents and business leaders, including me. It was a victory of sorts.

The shelter, named John Heuss House, after a past rector of Trinity Church, was going to open in mid-December. Our first advisory board meeting was held a week before. At that meeting Winfield Peacock, a Presbyterian minister who had worked with the homeless and was going to run the shelter, told us something we hadn't known before: Since city-run dormitory shelters are too big to control adequately, a new concept was being introduced. "Drop-in centers" would be smaller facilities that provided meals, clothes, but no beds. The aim was to help the homeless without disrupting neighborhoods. By catering to fewer people, the "drop-ins" would be manageable. And John Heuss House was to be a drop-in center.

All that sounded pretty good.

Winfield Peacock spoke eloquently about the work they were doing for the homeless, the most fragile members of the community, as he called them. "We don't use a social-work model. Our model is the Cross. These people are not 'cases' to be monitored, or 'problems.' They are children of God."

All at once I was feeling guilty—really guilty. Mary had accused me of not being Christian. But what else had she said? *It's not too late to change your thinking—reverse the negatives and make them positive.* Could I?

After the meeting I went up to Peacock. "Look, Reverend," I blurted out, afraid if I hesitated I wouldn't say anything, "I fought you and lost. Now. . . uh. . .er. . .what can I do for you?"

Had he been sitting on a chair, I think the minister would have fallen off it.

"I'm serious," I said, feeling curiously happy. "I'm putting Delmonico's at your service. We want to make sure this center is successful, a model program."

The day the drop-in center opened, I walked over, half expecting to see a line of the homeless outside. There was none. Venturing down the steps into the center, I saw people quietly reading, watching television, talking to counselors. Win Peacock hurried over with a smile, extending a hand of welcome.

Within a few days we began making early-morning deliveries of day-old food, good food that in the past we wasted. And when the center's meat slicer went on the blink, we told them to come and use Delmonico's. When their dishwasher broke, we sent our mechanic to fix it and do a survey of all their equipment. When I told one of our contractors to put repairs on our bill, he got indignant: "Naaah! I'll donate my costs. I can help the needy too, you know."

The goodwill became contagious. We businessmen continue to find ways to help our drop-in center and make the neighborhood better.

For years I'd heard my priest read these words of Jesus: "I was hungry and you gave me food, I was thirsty and you gave me drink, I was a stranger and you welcomed me, I was naked and you clothed me . . ." (Matthew 25:35–36 RSV).

As many times as I'd heard that passage, it had gone over my head— until I began doing my small bit to help the least of these, my brothers and sisters. Then I finally understood: Christ was talking about the people at our own drop-in center.

He was talking about the needy people in your neighborhood.

"YOU ARE HIM HERE"

by Quin Sherrer

Over a long period of time, many people in our church had made a project of helping a young teenage girl who lived in a detention home. At first she was rebellious, unresponsive. But they kept visiting her, taking clothes to her, bringing her into their homes for weekend passes. Mostly they loved her. And in the process they introduced her to their friend, Jesus.

One Sunday night soon after her release, she asked to speak before our church congregation. Glowing, she stood at the pulpit and said, "I want so much to thank Jesus for what He's done for me. But you are Him here. So I'll thank you."

So many times since then her words have echoed back at me. Whenever I've been asked to help someone else who has a problem, I hear again, "You are Him here."

Each of us will have at least one opportunity today to respond to someone as He would. Let's pray that we won't fail.

JESUS IN EACH ONE OF THEM

by Paul Brand, MD

The caste system in India is pervasive. . . .

The lowest stratum of society is the deformed leprosy patient. Doctors, lawyers and priests are looked upon as the highest stratum, and are treated with great deference. I have often been embarrassed by the way patients will bow to the ground and touch my feet before I have a chance to stop them.

In our leprosy sanitarium at Karigiri in South India we have a lovely chapel, made from stones that have been hewn from the surrounding rocky hills. In that chapel during the season of Lent, we have an early morning communion service every Wednesday. It is open to Christian staff and patients, and is led by one of the doctors who is also an ordained presbyter of the Church of South India. The numbers are few at that early hour, and we stand in a circle around the table, passing the bread and the wine from hand to hand. In turn, we speak the name of the person to our left, and use the scriptural words that define the elements that we share.

On the day I remember best, the person to my right was a leprosy patient, Manikam, a beggar on whose deformed hands I had operated a few weeks before. He had come to know the Lord, and was happy both in the improvement in his hands and in his new faith. In the hospital ward, however, it was still difficult to get him to look at the doctors as he responded to our questions. His downcast eyes still identified him as an outcast.

As the plate with the bread came around the circle, Manikam took his piece, and then took the plate to pass it to me. Because his hands were still stiff from the recent surgery and plaster cast, as well as from the effect of his previous disease and injuries, he fumbled and almost dropped the plate. I reached out to steady it for him. Then he turned to me and held out the bread. His back was straight, his voice was clear and strong and his eyes looked directly into mine. "Paul," he said, "This is the body of Christ, broken for you." As I took the bread my eyes misted over, and I could hardly control my voice as I turned to pass the bread to the person on my left.

I cannot describe the delight I felt as I looked into Manikam's face and recognized the life of Jesus as he spoke the words, "The body of Christ, broken for you." It was as though my eyes had been opened and I saw a new person. Jesus had broken hands, Jesus knew pain and rejection, and it was Jesus whose life and death had brought about the sense of love and fellowship that I experienced with my patient at that time. We were one loaf, one body, and shared one Lord.

This was a miracle. Anywhere but in that situation, and anytime in the past, he would have called me "Doctor Brand." And in a humble voice, with downcast eyes. To hear my name, Paul, ring out in the chapel, with the freedom and confidence of an equal member of the same body, was a most moving thing. All of us must have felt the transformation. We thanked God for the reality behind the symbol of the broken bread, broken from the one loaf. . . .

When I take the bread, I try to be thankful for three aspects of that broken bread that have significance for me. First I remember the sacrifice of Jesus on the cross, when His body was broken for me. Then I think of the way in which His life continues to sustain me today; His body, the Living Bread.

Then I look around me and recognize those who are worshipping with me. I need to remind myself of our essential oneness, and I do it individually. Deliberately downplaying our differences, I seek to see Jesus in each one of them. That way it becomes indeed a love feast as well as a memorial service and, not least, a celebration of the continuing life of the Lord within me.

JESUS IN HER EYES

by Betty Graham

I don't know anyone who loves children more than my sister Hazel. She just bubbles whenever she is near any small child. No one could have been more thrilled than she was when her first son arrived. And the children she comes in contact with are drawn to her like pins to a magnet. She doesn't do anything special, but they seem to sense something that makes them want to be around her.

I used to wonder what that special something was, until one morning I watched her feed cereal to her two-year-old son Bobby. She was talking to him with each bite, the same as I did with my own children. But all of a sudden Bobby put his finger on Hazel's magic. He stopped eating and pointed at his mother. "Mommy," he said, "I see Jesus in your eyes."

When we truly love someone, it can't be hidden. It shines out in our eyes for all to see. When Christ is in your heart, His love shines out to the world. Bobby saw Christ's love in Hazel's eyes.

What reflects in my eyes today, and in yours? Are we letting God speak to others through us? Or by our actions, are we turning Him away? We can let His love shine out, just by letting those around us know we care.

EYES OF FAITH

by Virginia Lively

When friends ask how I first discovered that my hands have been given a ministry of healing, I'm sure they don't expect to hear the kind of story that I am about to set down. Apparently the fact that I am a suburban housewife who saves grocery stamps and has to watch her weight seems a poor beginning to a story of divine intervention.

It started the year my father entered the tuberculosis sanitarium in Tampa, Florida. We had long since given up hope. He was too old for an operation and we had seen the X-rays. The last thing on earth that would have occurred to any of us—Mother or my sister or me—was to ask God to step in and change medical facts.

And yet my husband Ed and I were active church members. As a banker, Ed was head of fund-raising, our two children went to Sunday school and I belonged to all the usual groups. We were, in short, typical, civic-minded churchgoers. Which is why the tears, when they began, caused us so much embarrassment.

It was in October, driving home from a PTA meeting, that I suddenly began to cry. I was in charge of the Halloween carnival that year, and at the meeting there had been some criticism of the plans. When I was still crying at bedtime, Ed put his arms around me and said, "Honey, all the carnivals in the world aren't that important."

But it wasn't the carnival. Even as I cried I knew that those tears were for something far bigger. I cried myself to sleep and in the morning, as soon as I opened my eyes, the tears started again. I choked them back while I fixed breakfast. But as soon as Ed and the children left, I burst into tears again.

This incredible state of affairs lasted four days. I took to wearing dark glasses even in the house so that my family would not guess how constantly I was crying. I was sure I was having a nervous breakdown.

It was on the morning of the fourth day, after Ed and the children had left, that a curious change took place. I saw nothing. I heard nothing. Yet all at once there was power in the air around me. The atmosphere itself seemed to hum and crackle as though I stood in the center of a vast electrical storm. As I try to put it into words it sounds fantastic, but at the time there was no sense that something beyond the possible was taking place.

I had sunk into the high-backed chair in the living room when suddenly through the window I saw the eastern horizon. Trees and houses stood between me and it, but I seemed to see right beyond to the place where earth and sky came together. And there, where they met, was a ball of light.

The light was moving, traveling toward me with amazing speed. It appeared white, yet from it poured all the colors I had ever seen.

And then it was beside me. Although it seemed impossible that anything with such energy could hold still, it took a position at my right shoulder and there it stayed. And as I stared, I started to smile. I smiled because He was smiling at me. For I now saw that it was not light, but a face.

How can I put into words the most beautiful countenance I have ever seen? "He is perfect" was the first thought that came. His forehead was high, His eyes exceptionally large. But I could never fix the color of His eyes any more than I could the color of the sea.

More, much more, than individual features was the overwhelming impression of life—unhampered life, life so brimming over with power and freedom that all living things I had seen till then seemed lumps of clay by comparison.

Not for a moment did I hesitate to call this Life at my side Jesus. And two things about Him struck me most. The first was His humor. I was astonished to see Him often break into outright laughter. And the second was His utter lack of condemnation. That He knew me down to my very marrow—knew all the stupid, cruel, silly things I had ever done—I realized at once. But I also saw that none of those things, or anything I would ever do, could alter the absolute caring, the unconditional love, that I saw in those eyes.

I could not grasp it. It was too immense a fact. I felt that if I gazed at Him for a thousand years I could not realize it all.

I did not have a thousand years; I had three months. For as long as that, the face of Jesus stayed beside me, never fading, never withdrawing. Many times I tried to tell someone else what I saw, but the words would never come. And meanwhile I carried on with my tasks—meals and shopping and the PTA with its carnival—but effortlessly, scarcely knowing I was doing them, so fixed were my thoughts on Him.

At the same time, I had never seemed so aware of other people. (How this was possible when my mind was full of Him alone I don't know, but it was true.) My husband, especially. Far from feeling that a third person had entered our marriage, I felt that Christ was the marriage, as though all along He had been the force drawing us together.

And the Bible! All at once I couldn't read enough of it. It was like tearing open a letter from someone who had known this Presence as a flesh-and-blood person, full of just the kind of specific details I longed to hear. Certain passages in particular had a strange effect on me. When the Bible described Jesus healing someone, the actual print on the page seemed to burn. The hand that touched it tingled as if I had touched an electric current.

And then one afternoon before the children got home, I was sitting, just looking at Him, when all of a sudden, in a patch of sunlight on the wall, appeared the X-ray of my father's chest. It was all scar tissue and cavities. Then as I watched, a white mist moved slowly up the wall. When it passed the diseased tissue, there appeared on my wall a picture of a healthy lung.

"Then Dad's well!" I said aloud, and at that the Person at my side burst into peal after peal of joyous laughter, which said that wholeness was always God's way.

I thought my heart would burst as I waited for the next Wednesday's X-ray. I enjoyed the scene in my mind again and again, imagining the ring of the telephone and Mother's voice stammering with excitement, "Darling—the most amazing—the most glorious—"

But when Mother called, her voice was flat. "The most annoying thing, Virginia. They got the slides mixed up! Poor Dad's got to go back for X-rays tomorrow. Why, they sent down pictures of someone who never even had TB. . . !"

But, of course, the next day's X-rays showed no sign of disease either; Dad was healed and lived out his long life in thanksgiving to God.

And it was Dad's healing that convinced me I must try to describe the indescribable that had happened to me. I went to an elderly pastor whom I had known a long time. To my astonishment he understood me at once. He gave me some books that recounted fairly similar things.

Then he said the words I have wished unsaid so many, many times. "Don't be surprised, Virginia, if the vision fades after a time. They usually do, you know."

Fade! I thought, as I drove home with that joyous Presence beside me. *Oh, it can't, it mustn't!* For the first time in the whole unbelievable experience my attention veered from Him to myself. And in that instant the vision was diminished, it actually disappeared for a second or two, though right away the radiant face was beside me again.

But the damage was done. The seed of self-concern was sown. The bright Presence would sometimes be missing for an hour or more. The more worried I got, the more self-centered I grew. *What have I done? What will I do without Him?* When He did return there would be no accusation in His eyes, just a tremendous compassion, as though He realized how difficult it had become for me to see Him.

At last all that was left of this experience was the strange tingling in my hands as I read the Bible stories of healing. One day I was visiting a friend in the hospital. She was hemorrhaging and in pain. On an impulse I reached out and touched her. My hand began to burn just as it did during the Bible-reading. My friend gave a little sigh of comfort and fell asleep. When the doctor examined her, he found that the hemorrhaging had stopped.

Over the next eight years there were dozens, scores of experiences of that kind, all as inexplicable as the first. And yet for me they were still years of emptiness and waiting. "I will always be with you," He had said when I last saw Him.

"But how will I know if I can't see You?" I called to Him, for He had seemed so far away.

"You will see Me," He said, and then He was gone.

But the years went by and the vision had not come back. And then one day, while speaking to a church group, I saw those love-lit eyes smiling once again into mine. I looked again. The eyes belonged to a lady in the second row. Suddenly the room was full of Him; He was in the eyes of everyone there. "You will see Me. . . ."

I used to wonder what would have happened if the old pastor had never spoken of the vision fading. Might I have had it forever? I think not. I think that the days when Jesus was real to my eyes were the days of the "childhood" of my faith, the joyous, effortless time of discovery. But I do not think He lets it stay that way.

He didn't for His first disciples; He doesn't for us today. He gives us a glimpse only. Perhaps He let me look so long because I am slow to learn. But, finally, He takes away all sensory clues. He is bigger than our eyes and ears can make Him, so He gives us instead the eyes of faith, and all humankind in which to discover His face.

A PILGRIM'S ASCENT

by Eleanor V. Sass

S ome years ago while touring Quebec, Canada, I visited the church of St. Anne de Beaupré where there is a staircase called the Scala Santa (Holy Stairway). It is a replica of a staircase in the Basilica of St. John Lateran in Rome, and that, in turn, is said to be a copy of the stairway Jesus ascended on His way to meet Pilate before His trial.

A guide told me that many pilgrims climb this stairway on their hands and knees, pausing for prayer at each step. "A form of penance," he said. I began to wonder what it would mean to me, a Protestant, if I did the same as those pilgrims. On impulse, I decided to try.

I knelt down on the first step. There I prayed for a safe journey for my parents who were going on vacation the next week. I moved up to the second step. I prayed for a cousin in the hospital. By the tenth step my knees were getting sore. I prayed for two friends who were having marital difficulties. By the twentieth step my hands were red and hurting a little from the slippery hardwood, but now I was praying for all unemployed people who couldn't find work.

At last I reached the top. At this point I was praying for world peace. I sat down on the twenty-eighth step and thought about the experience, and how the scope of my prayers seemed to have expanded. I hadn't climbed the staircase to put myself in the shoes of Jesus, as some people had, or to share His pain. I wasn't in pain, or tired. I felt exhilarated.

Ever since, the memory of those twenty-eight steps has helped me to extend and deepen my prayer life. Perhaps you too might benefit from trying this discipline from time to time: Picture yourself on a staircase, praying at each step, letting your prayers grow as you ask the Lord to be with specific people, and eventually, whole groups—even whole governments of people. Maybe you won't make it to the twenty-eighth step (I seldom do) but I can tell you this: The higher you climb, the closer you'll feel to God!